Unique International Recipes
Volume 1

Rinaldi di Asiago

Publisher
2020:Marketing Communications LLC

2020:Marketing Communications LLC

Unique International Recipes
Volume 1

Author: Rinaldi di Asiago

Copyright 2010
By 2020:Marketing Communications LLC

ISBN: 978-0-557-30325-0

ALL RIGHTS RESERVED. No part of this book covered by copyright may be reproduced in any way in print, broadcast, or on the internet. For any permissions, send requests in writing to marketing2020@aol.com

Disclaimer

This publication is intended to provide accurate information regarding selected recipes from 13 countries around the world, including ingredients and preparation instructions. However, due to the number of sources involved, issues arising from translating non English recipes to English and the fact that recipes are qualitative guides, guarantees of complete accuracy are not possible. In addition, weights and measures used in many countries vary from those used in the USA.

Recipe Table of Contents

1. Africa 4

2. Australia 29

3. Caribbean 43

4. France 58

5. Germany 78

6. Greece 95

7. India 115

8. Ireland 137

9. Israel 153

10. Middle East 159

11. Morocco 185

12. Philippines 197

13. Russia 211

14. USA 237

Part 1: African Recipes

Home to hundreds of tribes and ethnic groups, there is a great deal of diversity in African cuisine-- in the use of basic ingredients as well as the manner of preparation and cooking techniques. A variety of recipes are presented in this book for the reader to sample a variety from different countries.

`The African kitchen is traditionally outside or in a separate building apart from the sleeping and living quarters. By far the most traditional and to this day the most common sight in an African kitchen is a large swing black pots filled with meat, vegetables, and spices simmering over a fire. The pot usually sits on three stones arranged in a triangle, and the fire slowly consumes three pieces of wood that meet at a point under the pot.

African Almond Chicken (Libya)

Ingredients
- 3 lb. whole chicken
- 1 pkg frozen peas
- 2 cups chicken stock
- 1 TB sherry
- ½ cup chopped almonds
- 1 cup diced celery
- salt to taste
- 3 TB Vegetable oil

Preparation
- Boil chicken in water until tender - about 30 minutes. Take out and set aside to cool. Save 2 cups of the chicken stock.
- Debone the cooled chicken. Oil. Then add the celery, peas, chicken stock, almonds, salt and sherry. Simmer 10 minutes.
- Thicken sauce with 2 TB cornstarch mixed in ¼ cup water. Add to sauce and bring to a boil until it thickens. Serve with noodles or a bowl of steaming rice. Serves 4.

Creme Caramela (Sudan)

Ingredients
- 8 Eggs
- 1 qt milk
- ½ cup sugar
- 2 TB melted butter
- 1 TB vanilla or banana extract if available
- ½ cup sugar
- Maraschino (or candied) cherries

Preparation
- In a 2-quart bowl beat eggs with milk and sugar until mixture is frothy. Add butter and extract.
- In a 1½-quart (6-cup) star-shaped aluminum cake pan melt ½ cup sugar and burn to caramel stage. Rotate the pan to spread caramel all around the sides. Beat the egg mixture again.
- Pour it quickly into the cake pan. Cover the pan with aluminum foil which has been well buttered on the under side. Place the pan in a larger pan half

filled with water (as you would do custard). Bake at 350 F for 30 minutes.
- Remove cover and test with a silver knife (when it comes out clean, custard is done). Chill until thoroughly cold. Turn the Caramela out onto a 10 to 12-inch platter. Garnish with cherries top and sides. Serves 6-8.

Accra Banana Peanut Cake (Ghana)

Ingredients
- 1 ¼ cups softened butter
- 2 cups sugar
- 4 beaten eggs
- 4 cups flour
- ¼ cup cake flour
- 1 tsp salt
- 4 tsp baking powder
- ½ tsp baking soda
- 8 mashed bananas
- ½ cup coarsely chopped peanuts
- ½ cup sugar
- 1 tsp cinnamon

Preparation
- In a large bowl, cream together the butter and sugar. Add the eggs and beat to combine.
- In a separate bowl, stir together the flour, salt, baking powder, and baking soda. Stir the flour mixture into the butter mixture alternately with the bananas and peanuts. Pour the batter into the prepared pan and bake for 30 minutes, or until a wooden skewer inserted in the center comes out clean.
- Remove from the oven and allow to cool on a wire rack. Stir together the ½ cup sugar and cinnamon.
- Sprinkle the sugar mixture over the top of the cake as soon as you remove it from the oven. Makes 1 - 9x13 cake.

African Banana Peanut Cake

Ingredients
- 2 cups all-purpose flour
- 2 tsp baking powder
- ¼ tsp salt
- ¼ tsp baking soda
- ⅔ cups butter (or margarine) softened
- ¾ cups sugar

- 2 eggs
- 4 large (about 2 cups) very ripe bananas--peeled and mashed
- 1 cup divided salted peanuts, coarsely -chopped

Preparation
- Combine flour, baking powder, salt and baking soda. Cream softened butter and sugar until light and fluffy; beat in eggs.
- Add dry ingredients alternately with mashed bananas just until combined; stir in 1/2 cup chopped peanuts. Scrape batter into well- greased 9x5 loaf pan; sprinkle top evenly with remaining chopped peanuts.
- Bake in 350 degree F oven 60 to 65 minutes or until toothpick inserted in center comes out clean. Cool in pan on wire rack for 10 minutes; turn out of pan and cool completely.
- Wrap in plastic wrap or foil. Cake is best if served next day. Yields 6 to 8 servings.

African Vegetarian Stew

Ingredients
- 4 small kohlrabi, peeled and cut into chunks
- 1 large chopped onion
- 2 sweet potatoes, peeled and cut into chunks
- 2 sliced thick zucchini
- 5 fresh tomatoes-- (or 16 oz. can)
- 1 15 oz. can garbanzo beans and liquid
- ½ cup couscous (or bulgar wheat)
- ¼ cup raisins
- 1 tsp ground coriander
- ½ tsp ground turmeric
- ½ tsp ground cinnamon
- ½ tsp ground ginger
- 5 TB ground cumin
- 3 cups water

Preparation
- Combine all the ingredients in a large saucepan. Bring to a boil, lower the heat, and simmer until the vegetables are tender, about 30 minutes. Serve the couscous separately, if desired.

Apricot-Fig Blatjang

Ingredients
- ¾ lb dried apricots (1 1/2 cups)
- ¼ lb dried figs (about 1/2 cup)
- ¼ lb golden raisins (about 1/2-cup)
- 1 small diced small onion
- ½ cup cider vinegar
- ¼ cup blanched almonds
- 1 TB minced fresh ginger
- 1 tsp red minced (or green chile pepper)-- of your choice
- Salt and cracked-white pepper to taste
- ¼ cup lemon juice-- about 1 lemon

Preparation
- In a saucepan, combine the apricots, figs, raisins, onion, and vinegar with enough water to just cover.
- Bring to a boil, reduce the heat, and simmer for 15 to 20 minutes, stirring frequently, until the mixture is about the thickness of honey (do not overcook, as the mixture will thicken as it cools). Remove from the heat.
- Meanwhile, toast the almonds on a backing sheet in a 325F oven for 8 to 10 minutes, or until just lightly browned.
- In a food processor or blender, combine the ginger, chile peppers, almonds, and salt and pepper to taste, and puree well.
- Add the pureed spice mixture and the lemon juice to the apricot mixture and stir well.

Baked Plantain on the Shell

Ingredients
- 4 large ripe plantains
- ½ cup brown sugar
- ¾ tsp cinnamon
- ¼ cup melted butter (or margarine)

Preparation
- Preheat oven to 350 degrees. Wash plantains and cut in half lengthwise. Do not peel.
- Arrange in a shallow baking dish with cut sides facing up.

- In a small bowl, combine brown sugar, cinnamon, and melted butter and stir well. Top plantains with brown sugar mixture.
- Cover pan and bake for 35 minutes or until plantains are soft. Serves 4.

Bamia
(Meatball and Okra Sauté in Tomato Sauce)

Ingredients
MEATBALLS
- 1 lb ground beef
- 1 beaten egg
- ¼ cup bread crumbs
- 3 Put thru press cloves garlic

OKRA
- ¼ cup corn oil
- 1 large chopped onion (1 cup)
- 1 ½ lb fresh okra (the smallest-size avail able)
- 2 TB (generous) tomato paste
- 2 cups boiling water
- ¼ tsp allspice

Preparation
- Mix meatball ingredients together thoroughly and form miniature meatballs 3/4-inch in diameter. Set aside. You will need only 8 to 10 meatballs for dish. The rest of meatballs may be refrigerated or frozen.
- In a pan, heat oil. Add onion and sauté over moderate heat until onion turns golden.
- Add okra and stir-fry over low heat for 5 minutes. This will sometimes brighten color. In a measuring cup or bowl, dissolve tomato paste in water. Add mixture and allspice to okra pan.
- Bring to a boil and cook for 3 minutes. Add 8 to 10 meatballs and simmer for 10 minutes longer. Do not overcook since okra is notoriously mucilaginous. Serve warm with rice and other dishes.

Batata Bel Lamoun
(Golden Potato Soup)

Ingredients
- 1 large sliced carrot
- 3 sliced ribs celery w/leaves
- 6 cups water

- 1 TB corn oil
- 2 cloves garlic, finely chopped
- 2 lb potatoes, peeled and sliced
- 2 tsp salt or to taste
- ¼ cup lemon juice
- 2 crumbled cubes kosher chicken consommé
- ¼ tsp ground turmeric

Preparation

- In a processor, puree carrot and celery with 3 cups of the water. Into a large pan, pour puree and remaining 3 cups of water. In a skillet, heat oil.
- Add garlic and stir-fry over low heat for 2 minutes, or until garlic begins to change color. Add the garlic to soup pan. Bring soup to a boil over moderate heat and skim off and discard any foam that accumulates.
- Add potatoes and cook over low heat for about 45 minutes. The potatoes will begin to disintegrate. At this point, remove pan from the heat and mash potatoes in pan with a hand masher or ricer.
- Bring soup to a boil again; add salt, lemon juice, consommé cubes, and turmeric. Simmer over low heat for 1/2 hour longer, stirring frequently to prevent potatoes sticking to pan. The soup will have turned a golden color.
- Adjust salt and lemon juice, if a more intense flavor is desired. Serve hot in a soup plate with as much rice as wanted. Serves 6.

Beef Brochettes

Ingredients

- 2 lb steak, bite sized pieces
- ½ large onion, chopped finely
- 10 sprigs parsley, chopped
- 1 tsp salt
- ¼ tsp black pepper
- 2 tsp paprika
- 1 tsp cumin
- 1 TB vinegar
- 1 TB olive oil
- 4 TB tomato paste
- 1 tsp salt
- 2 tsp olive oil
- ½ tsp Tabasco sauce (more if desired)
- 4 TB vinegar
- 2 TB water

Preparation
- Mix well all ingredients in a large mixing bowl. Refrigerate at least 8 hours or overnight, if possible. When ready to cook, spear 5 or 6 pieces of meat on each skewer.
- Broil meat over a charcoal fire until done to your liking. Serve with large chunks of French bread.
- Hot Sauce: Blend tomato paste and olive oil in bowl. Mix thoroughly. Add vinegar, salt, Tabasco and water. Mix well. Add more Tabasco for hotter taste. Refrigerate until ready to use.

Beef Stew (Gambia)

Ingredients
- 2 lb cubed lean stew meat
- 1 can tomatoes (28 ounce)
- 1 bell pepper, cut in strips
- 1 celery stalk, slice diagonally
- 1 cubcd potato
- 1 large carrot, sliced diagonally
- 1 yellow onion, sliced
- 1 cubed sweet potato
- 1 tsp salt
- 6 TB tomato paste
- ½ tsp cayenne pepper
- ½ cup creamy peanut butter
- ½ cup thawed frozen peas

Preparation
- Combine the beef, tomatoes, bell pepper, celery, potato, carrot, onion sweet potato, salt and tomato paste in a 5-quart saucepan, and mix well.
- Bring to a boil, reduce heat, and simmer, covered, for 1 hour, adding water if necessary. Stir in the cayenne pepper and peanut butter
- Simmer for 1 hour longer or until the vegetables and beef are tender.
- Add the peas, and simmer for 5 minutes. Ladle onto a large platter. Garnish with bell pepper slices and parsley. Serve over rice.

Beet Appetizer Salad

Ingredients

- 2 lb beets
- Salt
- ½ diced Spanish onion
- 4 diced tomatoes, skinned, seeded
- 2 chopped garlic cloves
- 4 TB chopped Italian parsley
- 4 TB chopped cilantro
- 4 medium boiled potatoes

DRESSING
- 2 TB vinegar
- 8 TB olive oil
- salt and pepper
- 1 hot red pepper

GARNISH
- black olives

Preparation
- Cut off ends of beets. Wash well and cook in boiling salted water until tender. Drain and remove skins under running cold water. Dice. Mix together the dressing ingredients.
- Combine beets in a salad bowl with the onion, tomato, garlic cilantro & parsley. Pour over half the dressing, toss gently & chill for 30 minutes. Slice the potatoes, place in a shallow bowl & toss with remaining dressing. Chill.
- When ready to assemble, arrange beets, tomato & onion in the centre of a shallow bowl and arrange potatoes in a ring around them. Garnish with olives. Serves 4.

Berbere

Ingredients
- 2 tsp whole cumin seeds
- 4 whole cloves
- ¾ tsp black cardamom seeds
- ½ tsp whole black peppercorns
- ½ tsp whole allspice
- 1 tsp fenugreek seeds
- ½ tsp whole coriander seeds
- 10 small dried red chilies
- ½ tsp grated ginger
- ¼ tsp turmeric
- 1 tsp salt
- 2 ½ TB sweet Hungarian paprika
- ⅛ tsp cinnamon

- ⅛ tsp ground cloves

Preparation
- In a small frying pan, on a low heat, toast cumin, cloves, cardamom, peppercorns, allspice, fenugreek & coriander for about 2 minutes, stirring constantly. Remove from heat & cool for 5 minutes. Discard stems from chilies.
- In a spice grinder or with a mortar & pestle, finely grind together the toasted spices & chilies. Mix in remaining ingredients. Store in refrigerator in a well sealed jar.

Bourek
(Beef-Stuffed Pastry Rolls)

Ingredients
- ¼ cup vegetable oil
- 1 small chopped (1/4 cup) onion
- ½ lb ground beef
- ½ tsp salt or to taste
- ¼ tsp black pepper
- 1 beaten egg
- 2 TB chopped flat leaf parsley
- 6 phyllo sheets, 12x17 each
- Lemon wedges for serving

Preparation
- When the fast of Ramadan is broken in the early evening hours, various dishes are considered a traditional part of the meal. This is one of those dishes.
- Heat 1 tablespoon of the oil in a skillet, add the onion and stir-fry over moderate heat for 2 minutes. Add the beef, salt and pepper and stir-fry for 5 minutes. Add the egg and parsley and fry for 1 minute more.
- Cool well. Take 1 phyllo sheet and spread it out flat with a short end nearest you. Place 2 heaping tablespoons of the beef mixture 2 inches in from the short edge.
- Fold both long sides in toward the middle, beginning with the short end roll the phyllo to shape a packet 4 inches long and 1 1/2 inches wide.
- Repeat with all the remaining phyllo sheets and stuffing. Set aside. Put the balance of the oil in a skillet over moderate/low heat and add the rolls.
- Brown on both sides for about 3 minutes; the low heat prevents the very thin pastry sheets from burning. Drain the rolls on paper towels for a

minute. Serve warm with a squeeze of lemon juice. Serves 6.

Casbah Moroccan Restaurant's Lamb & Okra Tagine

Ingredients
- ¾ lb leg of lamb (or shank)
- ¾ tsp salt
- ¾ tsp black pepper
- ½ cup olive oil
- 1 medium chopped onion
- 2 tsp ginger
- 1 pinch saffron or 1/2 tsp turmeric
- 2 medium tomatoes, peeled and cut into quarters
- water
- 3 TB chopped cilantro
- 2 TB chopped parsley
- 1 lb trimmed okra

Preparation
- Cut meat into 2-in. chunks; season with salt and pepper; set aside. Heat olive oil in large Dutch oven or skillet. Add onion, ginger, saffron, stirring until onion begins to turn translucent.
- Add meat and sauté briefly to brown, just a minute or two; then add tomatoes and water to cover and stir. Cover and simmer for 1 hour, or until meat is tender.
- Add cilantro, parsley, and okra and adjust water if needed. Simmer 10 minutes, until okra is just tender. Make sure okra remains whole. In a serving plate, place the meat first, then top with okra, and finally add the rest of the sauce on top. Garnish with more chopped parsley, if desired. Serve hot.

Chicken Stew (Ethiopia)

Ingredients
- 3 cups finely-chopped Bermuda onions
- ⅓ cup butter (or olive oil)
- ½ tsp cayenne pepper
- 1 tsp paprika

- ½ tsp pepper
- 1/4 tsp ground ginger
- 3 cups divided water
- 3 lb chicken cut in 1" pieces, including the neck and gizzard
- ¼ cup lemon juice
- 8 whole hard-boiled eggs, peeled

Preparation

- In a heavy 4 to 6 quart pot or Dutch oven, brown the onions, without using any fat, stirring constantly, until browned.
- Add the butter or oil, cayenne, paprika, pepper, ginger, and 1 cup of the water and stir to combine. In a bowl, combine the remaining 2 cups of the water and lemon juice.
- Put the chicken in a large bowl, pour the lemon juice mixture over the top, and let the chicken soak for 10 minutes. Drain the chicken, add it to the pot with the onions, and stir to combine.
- Simmer, covered, over low heat until the chicken is tender. Add more water if necessary. If the stew is too watery, mix 2 tablespoons flour with 2 tablespoons water and stir it into the stew. A few minutes before serving, add the eggs. Serves 8.

Egusi Soup

Ingredients

- ¾ cup egusi seeds
- 1 ½ lb beef tenderloin
- ¾ tsp salt
- ¼ tsp black pepper
- ¼ cup peanut oil
- 2 large chopped tomatoes
- 1 small onion, peeled and chopped
- 1 seeded and chopped chilies (or jalapeno peppers) (1-2)
- 1 can tomato sauce (8 oz.)
- ½ cup water
- 2 lb any combination of crab, shrimp, fish
- 1 lb fresh spinach, cleaned and finely chopped- OR 10 oz frozen chopped spinach, thawed

Preparation

- Place egusi seeds in a blender and blend for 30 to 40 seconds or until mixture is a powdery paste. Set aside. Wash beef and cut into bite-size cubes.

- Season with salt and black pepper. In a large frying pan, heat oil over medium-high heat for 4 to 5 minutes. Add beef and sauté for 3 to 5 minutes or until brown but not cooked through.
- Place tomatoes, onions, and peppers in a blender and blend for about 30 seconds or until smooth. Add tomato mixture to meat, reduce heat to medium-low, and cover. Cook for 1-1/2 to 2 hours or until meat is tender.
- Add tomato sauce, 1-1/2 cups water, crab, shrimp, and smoked fish and simmer for 10 minutes. Add spinach and ground egusi seeds and continue to simmer for 10 minutes more. Serve with fufu.

Egyptian Chocolate Cake

Ingredients
- 1 ¾ cups unbleached sifted flour
- 2 tsp baking powder
- 1 tsp ground cinnamon
- ⅛ tsp ground cloves
- 4 oz semisweet chocolate
- ½ cup brewed strong coffee
- ½ cup butter (or regular-margarine)
- 1 cup sugar
- 2 large eggs
- 1 tsp vanilla extract
- ½ cup milk

CINNAMON WHIPPED CREAM
- 2 cups heavy whipping cream
- ¼ cup sugar
- 2 tsp vanilla extract
- ½ tsp ground cinnamon

Preparation
- Sift the flour, baking powder, cinnamon and cloves together; set aside. Combine chocolate and coffee in small saucepan. Cook over low heat until the chocolate is melted, stirring constantly.
- Remove from heat and cool to room temperature. Cream the butter and sugar together in a mixing bowl, until they are light and fluffy. Use an electric mixer set on medium speed. Add eggs, one at a time, beating well after each addition.
- Beat in vanilla and chocolate mixture. Add dry ingredients alternately with milk to the creamed mixture, beating well after each addition. Pour batter into 2 greased and waxed paper-lined 8-inch cake pans.
- Bake in a preheated 350 degree F. oven for 30 minutes or until cake tests

done. Cool in pans on racks for 10 minutes. Remove from pans; cool completely on racks. To assemble the cake, place one cake layer on serving plate.
- Spread with Cinnamon Whipped Cream. Top with second cake layer. Frost sides and top with remaining Cinnamon Whipped Cream. Refrigerate until serving time.

  CINNAMON WHIPPED CREAM: Chill large mixing bowl and beaters.
- Combine cream, sugar, vanilla, and cinnamon and beat with an electric mixer set at high speed until soft peaks form and mixture is thick enough to spread. Do not over beat or you will have butter instead of whipped cream.

Egyptian Haroset

Ingredients
- 1 lb raisins
- 8 oz pitted dates
- 2 cups water
- ¼ cup sugar
- ¼ cup chopped walnuts (or pecans)

Preparation
- Cover raisins and dates with water; let stand 1 hr.
- Add the sugar and blend or food-process until roughly chopped.
- Transfer to a heavy saucepan and simmer 20 min or until fruits are cooked and water is absorbed. When cool, stir in chopped nuts.

Egyptian Kebabs

Ingredients
- 2 whole chicken breasts, skinned and boned
- 1 TB yogurt
- ¼ tsp salt
- ¼ tsp turmeric
- ⅛ tsp dry mustard
- 1/2 tsp curry powder
- ⅛ tsp ground cardamom
- 1 tsp lemon juice
- 1 tsp vinegar
- slices thin onion

- small tomatoes, halved

Preparation
- Cut each chicken into 16 squares. Combine with the yogurt, salt, turmeric, mustard, curry powder, cardamom, lemon juice and vinegar and let stand for 1/2 hour. Thread on skewers 2 chicken pieces, 1 slice of onion, 2 chicken pieces, 1/2 tomato.
- Repeat till all ingredients are used. Cook slowly, turning occasionally and brushing with the marinade, over hot coals OR under the broiler till the chicken is tender, about 10 minutes. Transfer to a hot platter, sprinkle with lemon juice and garnish with fresh tomatoes, green pepper rings and fresh mint or parsley.

Egyptian Pickled Turnips

Ingredients
- 2 kilos turnips
- 1 beetroot
- 7 cups water
- 3 ½ TB salt

Preparation
- Wash turnips and beetroot, scrub well and either slice or cut into quarters. Boil water with salt and put into pickling jar to cool. When tepid, add vegetables, cover and keep in warm place away from direct light.
- These pickles should be ready in about 48 hours. The purpose of the beet is to give the turnips a bright pink color, and they don't affect the flavor. You can toss it out once the turnips are pink, or leave them out entirely if you don't want colored turnips.

Salady Voankazo (Madagascar)
(Fruit Compote with Lichee Nuts)

Ingredients
- 1 cup fresh pineapple, cut into 1" pieces
- 1 cup fresh cantaloupe, cut into 1/2"pieces
- 1 cup peeled and thinly sliced oranges
- ½ cup sliced strawberries
- ½ cup canned lichee nuts
- ½ cup sugar
- ½ cup water

- ¼ tsp salt
- 2 TB lemon juice
- 2 TB vanilla

Preparation
- In a 2 quart bowl, combine the pineapple, cantaloupe, orange, and strawberries and stir to combine.
- Sprinkle the lichee over the top. In a small sauce pan, combine the sugar, water, salt, and lemon juice and stir to combine. Bring to a boil and boil hard for 1 minute.
- Stir in the vanilla. Pour the hot syrup over the fruit. Chill in the refrigerator for 1 hour. If you wish, when you serve the salad you can sprinkle a few drops of vanilla over individual servings. Serves 8.

Fufu

Ingredients
- 4 cups water
- 1 ¼ cups Cream of Wheat
- 1 cup potato flakes
- 1 TB margarine (optional)
- ⅛ tsp salt (optional)

Preparation
- In a small saucepan, bring 2 cups water to a boil over medium heat. Reduce heat to low. In a large saucepan, bring 2 cups water to a boil over high heat.
- Reduce heat to medium and add Cream of Wheat 1/4 cup at a time, stirring constantly. Add tablespoons of hot water from the other pan when mixture gets too thick to stir.
- Add potato flakes 1/4 cup at a time, stirring constantly and, when necessary, adding hot water. Add margarine and salt and stir until margarine is melted.
- Continue to cook, stirring vigorously, until fufu pulls away from the sides of the pan and forms a ball. Form fufu into cup-size balls and place on plates or in bowls. Makes about 3 cups fufu.

Ful Nabed
(Egyptian Bean and Vegetable Soup)

Ingredients

- 1 cup chopped onions
- 2 garlic cloves, pressed
- ¼ cup olive oil
- 1 tsp ground cumin seeds
- 1 ½ tsp sweet Hungarian paprika
- ¼ tsp cayenne
- 2 bay leaves
- 1 large chopped carrot
- 1 cup chopped fresh tomatoes
- 3 ½ cups vegetable stock
- 2 cups canned (cooked) fava beans
- ¼ cup chopped fresh parsley
- 3 TB fresh lemon juice
- freshly ground black pepper and salt to taste
- fresh mint leaves (optional)

Preparation

- In a large soup pot sauté the onions and garlic in the olive oil until the onions are translucent. Add the cumin, paprika, cayenne, bay leaves, and carrots and cook on medium heat for 5 minutes.
- Stir in the chopped tomatoes and vegetable stock and simmer until the carrots are tender, about 15 minutes. Finally, add the cooked fava beans and the parsley and lemon juice.
- Add salt and pepper to taste. Full Nabed can be served with Pita Bread and garnished with fresh mint leaves.

Hamam Mahshi
(Braised Pigeons & Fireek)

Ingredients

- 8 TB butter
- ½ cup finely chopped onion
- giblets of one pigeon, finely chopped
- 2 ½ cups Fireek (coarsely crushed green wheat grains)
- 2 tsp mint, fresh, finely cut or mint
- 1 tsp crumble dried mint
- 1 ½ tsp salt
- freshly ground black pepper
- 4 – 1lb pigeons, oven ready OR 4 – 1lb doves
- 1 baby young partridge

- 1 quail, woodcock, pheasant, or grouse
- 1 ½ cups cold water
- ½ cup fresh or canned chicken stock
- 1 parsley sprig

Preparation

- Over moderate heat melt 4 tablespoons of the butter in a heavy 10 to 12 inch skillet. When the foam begins to subside, add the onions and the pigeon giblets and, stirring frequently, cook for 8 to 10 minutes, or until the onions are soft and light brown.
- Add the fireek, mint, 1 teaspoon of the salt and a few grindings of the pepper and stir for 2 or 3 minutes until the grains are coated with butter. Set aside. Preheat the oven to 350 degrees (F). Pat the pigeons thoroughly dry inside and out with paper towels and sprinkle their cavities with the remaining salt and a few grindings of pepper.
- Then stuff 5 tablespoons of the fireek mixture into the breast cavity and 1 tablespoon into the neck cavity of each pigeon. Set the remaining fireek aside. Fasten the neck skin to the back of each bird with a skewer and close the breast openings by lacing them with skewers or sewing them with heavy white thread.
- Truss the birds by tying their legs together and brush the skins with the remaining 4 tablespoons of butter. Place the pigeons, breast side up, in a heavy 4 to 5 quart casserole and pour in the water. Bring to a boil on top of the stove, cover tightly and braise in the middle of the oven for 45 minutes.
- Baste the pigeons with the liquid in the casserole, and continue braising for 1 hour longer. To test for doneness, pierce the thigh of a bird with the point of a small, sharp knife. If the juices that run out are slightly pink, cook for another 5 to 10 minutes.
- A half hour or so before the pigeons are done, bring the chicken stock to a boil in a 2 to 3 quart saucepan over high heat. Stirring constantly, add the reserved fireek mixture and bring to a boil again.
- Reduce the heat to low, cover tightly, and simmer for 30 minutes, or until the grains are tender and have absorbed all the liquid. To serve, arrange the pigeons on a heated platter and remove the trussing strings and skewers.
- Moisten the pigeons with the liquid remaining in the casserole, and garnish the platter with parsley. Fluff the fireek with a fork and serve it separately in a heated bowl.

Lamb and Sausage Couscous

Ingredients

- 3 lb lamb shoulder cut into 2-in- cubes
- ½ tsp salt or to taste
- freshly ground black pepper
- 1 TB olive oil
- 1 medium onion, quartered
- 4 medium carrots, peeled and cut into ½ inch pieces
- 2 celery stalks cut into 4 pieces
- ¼ cup tomato paste
- 3 TB all-purpose flour
- 1 cup dry white wine
- 6 cups low-sodium chicken broth or water
- 1 tsp cayenne pepper
- 1 TB ground cumin
- 6 spicy sausages (preferably Merguez Sausage)
- 2 medium zucchini cut into rounds 1 inch thick
- 1 ½ cups couscous

Preparation

- PREHEAT OVEN TO 325F. Pat the meat dry and sprinkle with salt and pepper as desired. Heat the oil in a large covered casserole or Dutch oven over high heat on top of the stove.
- Add the meat, without crowding, in batches if necessary, and brown well on all sides. Remove pieces to a plate as they are done and reserve. Repeat until all meat is browned. Do not pour off fat. Replace the casserole over medium heat.
- Add the onion, carrots, celery and tomato paste. Cook, stirring occasionally, 5 minutes. Use your spoon to loosen and dissolve the brown bits stuck to the bottom of the casserole. Add flour and cook, stirring, an additional minute.
- Add wine, meat (and any juices on the plate), stock, cayenne and cumin. Cover, bring to a boil and place in the oven for 1 1/4 hours, or until meat is tender.
- Meanwhile, combine sausage and zucchini in an ovenproof dish, cover and place in the oven until sausages are cooked, about 20 minutes. Follow directions on the back of the box and cook the couscous.
- Remove stewed lamb and the sausage/ vegetable mixture from the oven. Using a slotted spoon, remove the meat from the sauce and place it in a serving bowl.
- Pour off and discard any excess fat from the sausages and add sausages

and vegetables to the lamb. Pour the thin gravy through a fine strainer into the serving bowl and discard the vegetables and spices that remain in the strainer.
- To serve, place the couscous in another serving dish. Pour the broth into a pitcher or soup tureen. Encourage guests to place couscous in their soup bowl, top with the meat and vegetables and moisten with soup.

Lamb Patties Moroccan Style with Harissa Sauce

Ingredients
- ½ lb ground lean lamb
- 1 tsp paprika
- ¼ tsp crushed dried hot peppers
- ¼ tsp ground black pepper
- 1 tsp ground cumin
- 2 tsp chopped garlic
- 2 TB grated onion
- 4 TB chopped parsley
- 1 salt to taste
- 1 TB vegetable oil
- 1 harissa sauce

Preparation
- Put the lamb in a mixing bowl and add all of the ingredients except the vegetable oil and harissa sauce. Blend the mixture thoroughly by hand.
- Shape the mixture into 8 equal size patties similar to hamburgers. Heat the oil in a non stick skillet large enough to hold all of the patties. Two pans may be necessary.
- Add the patties to the skillet. Cook them over medium high heat about 3 to 4 minutes on each side, depending on the degree of doneness desired. Drain on paper towels and serve with the harissa sauce on the side.

Lamb With Artichokes and Preserved Lemons

Ingredients
- 3 lb boneless lamb shoulder
- 1 small onion, chopped

- 2 garlic cloves, minced
- 1 ½ tsp ground ginger
- ½ tsp ground turmeric
- 1 tsp powdered saffron (optional)
- 3 TB vinegar
- 12 small wide artichokes
- 12 Moroccan preserved lemons
- ½ cup Kalamata olives
- 2 TB lemon juice (optional)

Preparation

- Trim fat off lamb. Cut meat into 1 1/2" chunks. In a 5-6 quart pan, combine lamb, onion, garlic, ginger, turmeric, and saffron. Cook, tightly covered, over medium heat for 30 minutes.
- Meanwhile, in a bowl combine vinegar and 1 quart water. Trim off stems, tough outer leaves, and sharp tips of artichokes, leaving pale, tender interior leaves. Cut in half lengthwise; scoop out and discard hairy chokes.
- As artichokes are trimmed, immerse in vinegar-water. After meat cooks 30 minutes, turn heat high, uncover pan, and stir often until juices evaporate and meat browns, 15-20 minutes.
- Stir in 2 cups water; simmer, covered, for 1 hour. Drain artichokes and add to lamb; simmer, covered, for 20 minutes. Add 8 preserved lemon quarters and olives; simmer, covered, until artichokes are tender when pierced, about 10 minutes longer.
- Add 2 tablespoons liquid from preserved lemons or lemon juice. Skim and discard fat from stew. Pour stew into a bowl and garnish with remaining lemon quarters. Serves 8.

Melokhia
(Egyptian Herb Soup)

Ingredients

- 125 gms dried melokhia leaves
- 1 kg fresh melokhia leaves*
- 1 ½ strong stock
- 1 salt
- 1 black pepper
- 25 gms olive oil
- 3 crushed garlic cloves
- 1 TB ground coriander
- ½ tsp cayenne pepper

Preparation

- Crush the dried melokhia leaves. Put them in a bowl and moisten with a little hot water. Set aside until they swell and double in bulk. If the leaves are not brittle enough to crumble, dry them out in a warm oven for a few minutes.
- If fresh leaves are being used, wash them thoroughly and cut off the stalks. Spread the leaves out on a clean cloth to dry. Chop them finely. Put the stock in a large saucepan (you can use any stock, except pork).
- Season with salt and pepper and bring to the boil. Add the chopped or crumbled leaves and simmer for 10 minutes if the leaves are fresh and for 30 minutes if dry. Meanwhile, prepare the "Taklia" or garlic sauce.
- Melt the butter in a small frying-pan. Add the garlic and fry, stirring, until it is golden brown. Add the coriander and cayenne and cook, stirring, for 2 minutes.
- Add the garlic mixture to the soup, cover the pan, and simmer for 3 minutes, stirring occasionally. Adjust the seasoning and serve.

Meni-meniyong (Mali)
(Malinese Sesame Honey Sweet)
(Makes about 40 pieces)

Ingredients

- 1 cup sesame seeds
- 1 cup honey
- 4 TB unsalted butter

Preparation

- Preheat oven to 450°F. Spread the sesame seeds on a baking sheet and toast in the oven for about 10-12 minutes. Remove and cool.
- Heat the honey and butter in a small saucepan over medium-low heat, stirring until it bubbles and darkens somewhat, about 3-5 minutes.
- Stir the toasted sesame seeds into honey mixture. Spread the mass onto a buttered baking sheet to a thickness of about 1/4 inch. Cool until it is just warm and cut into finger-sized pieces. Cool completely and serve.

Mtuzi wa Samaki (Kenya)
(East African fish in coconut curry)

Ingredients

- 2-2 ½ lb fish filets, cut into serving portions

- salt and pepper to taste
- 1 onion, chopped or sliced
- 2 red or green bell peppers, chopped or sliced
- 6-8 cloves garlic, minced
- 1 cup tomatoes, seeded and chopped
- 1 ½ cups coconut milk
- 2-3 tsp garam masala or curry powder
- 1-2 TB tamarind paste or lemon juice
- salt and pepper to taste

Preparation

- Heat the oil over medium-high flame in a large skillet or pot. Season the fish with salt and pepper. Sear the fish fillets on both sides and remove to a plate. Do not cook through.
- Reduce the heat to medium and add the onions and peppers. Sauté until the onion is translucent. Add the garlic and sauté 1-2 minutes more.
- Add the tomatoes, coconut milk, garam masala or curry powder, tamarind paste or lemon juice, salt and pepper. Bring to a boil, and then reduce heat to low and simmer for 6-8 minutes.
- Add the fish fillets, cover and continue to simmer until the fish is cooked through, 5-10 minutes. Serve with rice, ugali, boiled potatoes, boiled cassava or chapatti.

Milookhiyya
(Egyptian Green Herb Soup)

Ingredients

- 1 qt. fresh or can chicken stock
- 1 cup dried milookhiyya*
- 1 TB tomato paste
- 1 tsp salt
- freshly ground black pepper
- 2 tsp finely chopped garlic
- 2 tsp ground coriander
- 2 TB butter

Preparation

- *Milookhiyya is a spinach-like Egyptian herb picked clean and finely crumbled.
- In a heavy 3 to 4 quart saucepan, bring stock to a boil over high heat.
- Stir in the milookhiyya, tomato paste, salt and a few grindings of the pepper and reduce the heat to low. Stirring occasionally, simmer for about

20 minutes, or until the milookhiyya has dissolved and the soup is thick and smooth.
- With a mortar and pestle or the back of a spoon, mash the garlic and coriander to a smooth paste. In a small skillet, melt the butter over moderate heat.
- When the foam has almost subsided, add the garlic and coriander and, stirring constantly, cook for a minute or two until the garlic is lightly browned.
- Add the entire contents of the skillet to the soup and, stirring constantly, simmer for 2 or 3 minutes more. Taste for seasoning and serve at once from a heated tureen.

Monrovian Coconut Pie (Liberia)

Ingredients
- ¾ cups softened butter
- 1/2 cup sugar
- 2 beaten eggs
- 2 cups grated fresh *or* moistened package coconut
- 1 cup milk
- 1 tsp vanilla
- ¼ tsp baking soda
- pastry for one 9 inch two-crust pie

Preparation
- Preheat the oven to 350 degrees. Roll out half of the dough and line a 9-inch pie pan. Wrap the remaining dough with plastic and set it aside. Bake the pie shell for 5 minutes.
- In a medium sized bowl, cream together the butter and sugar. Add the eggs and beat to combine. Add the coconut, milk, vanilla, and baking soda and beat until thoroughly combined.
- Pour the filling into the partially baked pie shell. Roll out the remaining dough and cut it into 1-inch wide strips.
- Lay the strips in a lattice pattern on the pie and flute the edges. Bake for 40 minutes, or until golden-brown. Remove from the oven and allow to cool on a wire rack.

Moroccan Date Cake

Ingredients

- ½ cup butter
- ¼ cup sugar (or up to double amt.)
- 4 eggs
- 1 tsp baking powder
- 1 cup unbleached white flour
- 1 tsp cinnamon
- 1 tsp nutmeg
- ½ tsp ground cloves
- ½ cup milk
- ½ tsp pure vanilla extract
- 1 cup chopped dates, pitted
- ½ cup chopped walnuts
- fresh whipped cream

Preparation

- Preheat the oven to 325 F. Cream together the butter and sugar. Beat in the eggs. Combine the baking powder, flour, cinnamon, nutmeg, and cloves. Add the dry ingredients to the egg mixture, beating well.
- Mix in the milk and vanilla. Beat well. Add the chopped dates and walnuts and stir again to distribute them evenly. Butter and flour a 9-inch cake pan.
- Pour the batter into the pan. Bake for about 30 minutes, until a knife inserted into the center comes out clean. Serve with fresh whipped cream.

###

Part 2: Australian Recipes

Australian foods have come a long way since the original British influence during the early settling of Australia. Unique tastes from Down Under will leave you anxious to try the next recipe! Truly unique!

The Aborigines have been using Australia's natural food resources for the last 40,000 years. Bushfoods include deliciously tangy fruits from the rainforests, aromatic herbs from our woodlands, zingy pepperleaf and delicate snowberries from the southern highlands, spicy bush tomatoes from the desert, and lean rich game meats from kangaroo and emus.

Kangaroo, anyone?

Abon

Ingredients

- 2 tsp brown sugar
- 1 ¼ lb lean rump steak
- 3 tsp coriander
- 1 ½ tsp cumin
- ¼ tsp laos (galangal)
- 2 tsp lemon juice
- 4 medium chopped onions
- 1 medium onion, crushed
- 2 garlic cloves, crushed
- ½ cup santan (thick coconut cream)
- 2 curry leaves
- oil as required
- salt to taste

Preparation

- Boil the meat in sufficient water until the steak is cooked and almost disintegrating. Remove the meat from the stock and shred it.
- Mix the following ingredients and spices together thoroughly: Meat, crushed onion, garlic, coriander, cumin, Laos, brown sugar, lemon juice, salt.
- Fry the above mixture in a little hot oil on a high heat for approximately five minutes. Add the santan and the curry leaves turn the heat to medium and cook until everything is cooked and all fluid has evaporated.
- Remove the curry leaves. Fry the chopped onions in hot oil until they are brown and crisp. Mix the fried onions with the mixture prepared above.

Aussie Meat Pie Filling

Ingredients

- 1 steak, minced (ground beef)
- 1 onion, chopped fine
- 1 pinch mixed herbs
- salt and pepper
- gravy
- dripping (solid oil will do)
- plain flour
- water from the meat mix

Preparation

- Combine minced steak, onion, herbs, and salt and pepper to your taste. Boil in water until cooked.
- Make gravy. Melt a little dripping (solid oil will do) in a pan. Mix in plain flour until all fat is absorbed (it becomes crumbly). Slowly add water from the meat mix and stir over low heat. Continue to add water until thickened. (As thick or thin as you like).
- Mix meat and gravy for pie filling.

Orange/Ginger Shrimp on the Barbie

Ingredients

- 12 giant prawns, shelled and deveined, (heads and tails)
- ¼ cup butter
- 1 cup orange juice (freshly -squeezed)
- 2 TB sherry
- 1 tsp orange zest (grated)
- 2 green onion tops and whites, minced
- 1 tsp grated ginger root (freshly)

Preparation

- Soak a dozen long wooden skewers in water for 30 minutes. Then push skewers through prawns, lengthwise, from head to tail with only 1 to a skewer.
- Combine all ingredients in saucepan and cook over medium to low heat, stirring, until butter is completely melted. Dip skewered prawns in the orange sauce and position on oiled grill rack about 4 inches above the coals.
- Baste liberally with sauce and grill for 2 minutes. Turn the prawn over and baste again, cooking for another 2 minutes.
- Smaller prawn will be done at this point, but continue basting and turning larger prawn until they are pink and cooked through.
- Remove from heat immediately when done, as they will get tough of overcooked. Use any remaining sauce for a dip for the prawns.

Australian Chocolate Crackles

Ingredients
- 150 gms melted copha
- 2 ½ cups rice bubbles
- 60 gms coconut desiccated
- 15 gms cocoa
- artificial sweetener to taste

Preparation
- Mix dry ingredients. Add melted copha and mix well. Divide into 24 patty pan papers.

Baked Stuffed Mullet

Ingredients
- 2 large fat mullet
- 250 gms cooked spaghetti
- 1 onion
- 2 bay leaves
- 1 TB tomato paste
- 1 tsp sugar
- 1 garlic clove, chopped and crushed
- 1 small capsicum (green pepper),chopped
- 1 ½ TB chopped parsley
- 2 sticks celery, chopped finely
- ½ tsp ginger
- ½ tsp basil
- salt and pepper to taste
- Tabasco sauce
- 1 TB olive (or vegetable oil)
- oyster sauce (optional)

Preparation
- Prepare mullet for baking by removing backbone, leaving it flat, ready for stuffing, sewing or tying up. Make sure fish is cleaned, scaled and washed thoroughly with black parts rubbed off.
- Remove as many bones as possible. Combine stuffing ingredients and add oil. This keeps spaghetti workable (soft) with other ingredients.

- Fill fish with stuffing. Tie securely, use small skewers or sew up sides of fish where necessary. Place fish on oiled baking dish and place in hot oven.
- Reduce heat and cook slowly for 30-45 minutes, according to fish size. Test to see if cooked.
- When cooked, remove from oven and when cool enough to handle, remove string or other securing device. This fish can be glazed with gelatin or oyster sauce.

Aussie Blender Lemon Drink

Ingredients
- 2 lemons, thin skinned
- 45 ml caster sugar
- 560 ml water
- 1 egg
- 4 ice cubes
- mint sprigs

Preparation
- Wipe lemons, cut into pieces and place in blender. Add sugar and water and blend for 30 seconds. Wash egg and add, whole to the blender with the ice cubes.
- Replace lid and blend for further 30 seconds. Strain into a jug or glass, add ice if liked and decorate with mint sprigs.

Brawn

Ingredients
- 2 pig's trotters
- 1 ½ lb knuckle of veal
- 1 shin of beef
- 4 bay leaves
- 6 cloves
- ½ tsp peppercorns
- ½ tsp whole allspice
- 1 ds salt
- ½ cup vinegar

Preparation

- Halve pig's trotters and meat, put in saucepan and just cover with water, also add bay leaves, cloves, pepper-corns, allspice and salt. Let boil for 3 - 4 hours.
- When cooked take out meat and chop finely, remove all bones, strain liquid into a basin, add chopped meat and vinegar, pepper and salt to taste. Put over fire and let come to boil. Pour into basins to set.

Champagne Melon Cooler

Ingredients

- 4 cups champagne melon, chopped, seeds removed
- ½ cup orange juice
- ½ cup lemon juice
- ½ cup caster sugar
- sliced strawberries

Preparation

- Blend champagne melon, juices and sugar until smooth. Refrigerate covered for several hours. Serve topped with sliced strawberries.
- For the perfect afternoon picnic, simply freeze for 1/2 to 1 hour before packing.

Chile 'n' Cheese Breakfast Casserole

Ingredients

- 3 English muffins, split
- 2 TB butter (or margarine), softened
- 1 lb bulk pork sausage
- 4 oz can green chiles, drained and chopped
- 3 cups shredded cheddar cheese
- 11/2 cups sour cream
- 12 beaten eggs

Preparation

- Spread cut side of each muffin with 1 teaspoon butter, and place, buttered side down, in a lightly greased 13" x 9" x 2" baking dish.
- Cook sausage in a skillet until browned, stirring to crumble; Drain. Layer

half of each sausage, chilies, and cheese over muffins.
- Combine sour cream and eggs; pour over casserole. Repeat layers with remaining sausage, chilies, and cheese; cover and refrigerate 8 hours.
- Remove from refrigerator, and let stand at room temperature 30 minutes. Bake, uncovered, at 350 F degrees for 35 to 40 minutes. 8 servings.

Chive-Mustard Potato Salad with Sausage Skewers

Ingredients
- 14 oz cherry tomatoes, halved
- ½ finely sliced red onion
- Cos (Romaine) lettuce
- 2 lb canned new potatoes, drained (halved if large)
- 1 TB seeded mustard
- 300 ml light sour cream
- 1 bunch chopped chives
- lemon juice
- salt to taste
- cracked pepper
- 6 large gourmet sausages

Preparation
- Preheat grill or barbecue. Combine tomatoes, onion and lettuce in shallow bowl. Add potatoes. Combine mustard, sour cream and chives, and season to taste with lemon juice, salt and pepper.
- Bring sausages to boil in a pan of water. Drain immediately and thread onto soaked wooden skewers. Cut slits across each.
- Grill or barbecue for five minutes, browning on all sides. Toss the chive dressing into the potato salad. Serve with sausage skewers. Serves 4.

Dill Pickled Okra

Ingredients
- 1 Kg okra pods
SPICES
- a few celery leaves
- clove of garlic, peeled and split
- sprig dill

- 2 pimento slices

PICKLE SOLUTION
- 2 ⅔ cups water
- 1 ⅔ cups white vinegar
- 2 TB salt

Preparation
- Scrub okra, pack into 4 jars. In each jar insert the spices.
- In a saucepan bring the pickle solution to the boil. Stir well and pour boiling liquid over okra and seal tightly. Let stand 3 weeks before serving.

Dopiaza
(Meat and Onion Curry)

Ingredients
- 2 pounds jointed chicken or 1 ½ lb lean cubed meat
- 1 ½ lb finely chopped onions
- 4 garlic cloves, finely chopped
- ½ cup ghee (or oil)
- 150 ml plain yoghurt
- 1 ½ lb onions, thinly sliced
- 4 fresh tomatoes, halved
- 1 TB fresh parsley (or coriander or cilantro), chopped
- salt to taste

SPICES
- 6 cloves
- 1 brown cardamom
- 2 inches cinnamon stick
- ½ tsp ground ginger
- 1 tsp turmeric
- 1 tsp ground chiles (cayenne)
- 1 tsp garam masala

Preparation
- If using chicken, skin it and cut into joints. If using meat, remove fat, and cut into 1" cubes. Fry the finely chopped onions and garlic until golden in the ghee or oil. Fold in the spices and stir fry about 5 minutes.
- Combine mixture with meat or poultry, the yoghurt and a cup of water, and put it all into a casserole (Dutch oven). Place in a preheated oven at 350F and cook for 20 minutes (or longer if using beef).
- Add and mix in the raw thinly sliced onions and tomatoes, together with the coriander or parsley. Salt to taste. Raise heat to 425F and cook for a

further 40 minutes or so. Serves 4.

Kangaroo Tail Soup

Ingredients
- 1 lb kangaroo tail, cut into pieces
- 2 lb beef
- 3 carrots
- 3 onions
- 1 bunch herbs
- pepper and salt
- butter

Preparation
- Cut the tail into joints and fry brown in butter, slice the vegetables and fry them also. Cut the meat into thin slices and boil all for 4 hours in 3 quarts of water.
- Take out the pieces of tail, strain the stock, thicken it with flour, and put back the pieces of tail and boil up another 10 minutes before serving. Serves 8.

Lentil Tangine

Ingredients
- 1 lb lentils, picked over
- 4 large vine-ripened tomatoes, chopped
- 1 large onion, chopped fine
- ¼ cup olive oil
- 2 garlic cloves, chopped
- 1 tsp paprika
- ½ tsp white pepper
- 1 tsp salt
- 3 ½ cups water, plus more if needed
- 1 cup fresh parsley
- 1 cup fresh coriander sprigs, chopped

Preparation
- In a 4-quart saucepan, combine lentils, tomatoes, onion, oil, garlic, paprika, pepper, salt, and water, making sure that water covers lentils,

adding more if needed.
- Simmer lentil mixture, covered, over moderately low heat 45 minutes, or until lentils are tender. Stir in parsley and coriander and cook 1 minute more. Serves 4.

Parrot Pie

Ingredients
- 12 parakeets (small parrots)
- 3 slices of beef, cooked
- 4 rashes bacon
- 3 hard-boiled eggs
- parsley and lemon peel, minced
- pepper and salt
- beef stock
- puff pastry

Preparation
- Line a pie dish with the beef cut into slices. Over them place six of the parakeets.
- Dredge with flour, fill up the spaces with egg cut in slices and scatter over the seasoning.
- Lie the bacon, cut in small strips, next. Add the remaining parakeets and fill up with the beef. Season.
- Pour in stock or water to nearly fill the dish, cover with puff-pastry and bake for 1 hour. Serves 6.

Potato & Roasted Garlic Soup

Ingredients
- 2 large garlic heads, unpeeled
- 2 TB olive oil
- 2 medium onions, chopped
- 4 lb yellow-fleshed potatoes, like Yukon
- 8 cups water

SCALLION PUREE GARNISH
- ½ cup olive oil
- 2cups chopped scallion greens

Preparation

- On a flat surface, smash garlic heads, root ends up, with the palm of the hand to break up cloves, leaving peels intact. Put garlic on a sheet of foil and drizzle with 1 tbsp oil.
- Sprinkle garlic with salt and pepper to taste and wrap tightly in foil. Bake garlic in the middle of the oven at 400 F for 40 minutes or until very tender.
- Unwrap garlic carefully and let stand until cool enough to handle. In a bowl, squeeze roasted garlic out of cloves by squeezing one end, discarding the skin.
- In a kettle, cook onions in remaining tablespoon of oil over moderate heat until softened. Peel and cut potatoes into 1/2-inch pieces and add to kettle with water.
- Bring water to a simmer and cook potatoes, covered, stirring occasionally, until very tender, about 20 minutes.
- Transfer half of potatoes with cooking liquid to a bowl and in a blender, in batches, puree with garlic until smooth.
- Transfer mixture as pureed back to kettle, stirring, and season soup with salt and pepper. Pour soup into serving bowls; garnish each with 1/2 TB scallion puree. Serve with crusty bread. Serves 8.
- SCALLION PUREE: In saucepan heat 1/4 cup oil over moderate heat and cook scallions just until tender and bright green in color (do not let brown).
- In a blender, puree scallion mixture with the remaining 1/4 cup oil until smooth. Season pure with salt and pepper and let cool. Makes about 3/4 cup.

Ricotta Cheese & Watermelon

Ingredients

- 500g ricotta cheese
- 1 large lemon, juiced and rind grated
- 8 slices chilled watermelon
- salt
- fresh ground black pepper

GARNISH

- Watermelon seeds
- Lemon wedges

Preparation

- Combine cheese, lemon rind, juice, salt and pepper in a bowl. Mix well using a fork.

- Remove some of the seeds from the watermelon and roast in moderate oven 180C for 7-8 minutes. Allow to cool.
- Arrange watermelon slices on plates and add ricotta cheese mixture. Sprinkle roasted seeds over cheese and garnish with lemon wedges.

Roast Wallaby

Ingredients
- 1 wallaby
- 1 forcemeat
- milk
- butter

Preparation
- In winter the animal may be hung for some days, as a hare, which it resembles, but in summer it must, like all other flesh be cooked very soon after it is killed.
- Cut off the hind legs at the first joints and after skinning and punching, let it lie in water for a little to draw out the blood.
- Make good veal forcemeat and after well washing the inside of the wallaby, stuff it and sew it up. Truss as a hare and roast before a bright clear fire from 1 1/4 to 1 3/4 hours, according to size. It must be kept some distance from the fire when first put down, or the outside will be too
- Baste well, first with milk and then with butter and when nearly done dredge with flour and baste again with butter until nicely frothed.

Rock Melon Chicken

Ingredients
- 3 rock melons
- 6 chicken breast fillets
- plain flour
- 250gms sliced mushrooms
- 125gms bean sprouts
- 4 spring onions, chopped
- 2 TB sesame oil
- 1 TB oyster sauce
- 1 TB soy sauce
- 175 gms cashew nuts, unsalted
- fresh parsley, chopped

Preparation

- Halve the rock melons and remove the seeds. Scoop out the flesh with a melon baller, leaving about 2 cm of flesh lining the shells.
- Cut the chicken breasts into thin slices and coat with flour. Heat oil in a wok. Add soy and oyster sauces, and chicken, and toss for 3-4 minutes.
- Add mushrooms, bean sprouts and spring onions and toss gently for two minutes, then add melon balls and cashew nuts.
- Mix well and transfer to melon shells. Cover with foil, place in baking tray and cook in hot oven 200C for 10 minutes. Garnish with parsley and serve.

Sauteed Okra

Ingredients

- 500g okra pods
- ¼ cup butter, melted
- ¼ cup sherry

Preparation

- Wash okra, leaving stems on. Place over boiling water and steam for about 15 minutes or until tender.
- Eat with fingers, dipping okra into melted butter and wine, or pour butter-mixture over okra.

Stir Fried Kangaroo Strips
With Bok Choy and Chili Black Beans

Ingredients

- 400g kangaroo fillet, trimmed and sliced into thin strips
- 1 bunch baby bok choy, washed
- 2 tsp Birds Eye chilies, chopped
- 1 tsp shallots (not spring onions), chopped
- 1 tsp garlic cloves, chopped
- 1 tsp fresh green ginger, chopped
- 25 ml Chinese brown rice wine
- 1 TB black beans, drained and washed
- 150 ml light beef stock
- 50 ml soy sauce

- 1 tsp fish sauce
- 1 tsp freshly ground black pepper

Preparation

- Trim bok choy leaves, slice larger ones in half lengthways, leaving stalks attached.
- Heat oil in wok. Add shallots, 3/4 of chilies, 3/4 of garlic and ginger and sauté quickly for 30 seconds until aromatic.
- Add the brown rice wine and reduce until it thickens.
- Add black beans, stock, soy sauce, and bring to boil. Cook for five minutes then take off heat and set aside.
- Heat oil in a clean wok. Add the remaining garlic and chilies, then kangaroo strips. Toss quickly for a few seconds over high heat. Add the warm sauce and the bok choy leaves.
- Cook quickly for a few seconds until leaves are wilted. Season with fish sauce and freshly ground black pepper. Pile onto center of plate and serve immediately. Serves 4.

###

Part 3: Caribbean Recipes

Food plays a central role in family life and traditions in the islands. Cooks spend days preparing menu offerings for holidays, festivals, and special family gatherings. The cuisine of the Caribbean is a cultural patchwork quilt representing the bounty of the islands' lush tropical vegetation, combined with the one or more diverse groups of people that have lived there, including the original Carib and Arawak Indians, followed by the Spanish, British, French, and Dutch settlers, as well as Africans, who have had a profound influence on the food and cultural traditions of the islands. Later followed Indian and Chinese settlers, and travelers from the United States.

Caribbean Jerk Pork Roast

Ingredients
- 3 lb boneless pork loin roast
- 1 TB dried onion
- 1 TB onion powder
- 2 tsp thyme, crushed
- 2 tsp salt
- 1 tsp allspice, ground
- ½ tsp nutmeg, ground
- ½ tsp cinnamon, ground
- 2 tsp sugar
- 1 tsp black pepper
- 1 tsp red pepper

Preparation
- Pat roast with paper toweling. Blend seasonings and rub evenly over pork roast.
- Place in shallow pan and roast at 350F for 45-60 minutes, until internal temp registers 160 degrees.
- Remove from oven, let rest 10 minutes. Temperature will rise about 5 degrees upon resting. Slice and serve, or cool slightly, slice and wrap well to refrigerate. Serves 4.

Caribbean Pork With Pineapple Salsa

Ingredients
- 2 eight oz. cans juice-packed pineapple chunks, drained, coarsely chopped
- 1 red onion, finely chopped
- 1 tomato, chopped
- ¼ cup fresh lime juice
- ¼ cup fresh cilantro or chopped parsley
- 2 TB honey
- 1 lb well-trimmed boneless pork chops
- 1 tsp paprika
- 1 tsp ground ginger
- 1 tsp ground allspice
- 1 tsp cinnamon
- ¾ tsp salt

- 2 tsp vegetable oil

Preparation

- In a medium bowl, combine the pineapple, onion, tomato, lime juice, cilantro, and honey. Set aside.
- Place the pork between 2 sheets of waxed paper and, with the flat side of a small skillet or meat pounder, pound the pork to a 1/8-inch thickness.
- In a sturdy plastic bag, combine the paprika, ginger, allspice, cinnamon and salt. Add the pork to the bag, tossing to coat.
- In a large nonstick skillet, heat the oil until hot but not smoking over medium heat. Add the pork cutlets and cook until browned and cooked through, about 3 minutes per side.
- Divide the pork cutlets among 4 plates and serve with the pineapple salsa. 4 servings

Caribbean Sweet Lime Salsa

Ingredients

- ¼ cup sugar
- 1 TB water
- 1 cup Rose's lime juice
- 2 small limes, thinly sliced
- 2 tsp Caribbean jerk spice
- 2 tsp rice wine vinegar

Preparation

- Put the sugar and water in a small saucepan over a moderate heat. Cook until the sugar caramelizes to a light golden brown.
- Carefully add the lime juice, limes, jerk spice and rice wine vinegar. Cook over a low heat for 15 minutes. Cool and serve at room temperature.

Bahamian Lobster "Buena Vista"

Ingredients

- 4 boiled lobsters
- 1 onion, chopped
- 1 garlic clove, finely chopped
- 2 tsp parsley, chopped

- 2 oz. brandy
- few drops of Tabasco
- 4 cups white sauce (see below)
- 1 cup sliced mushrooms
- salt and pepper
- ½ cup bread crumbs
- 2 tsp Worcestershire sauce

Preparation

- Halve the lobsters. Remove the meat and dice. Wash the shells and retain. In a saucepan, melt some butter; add the onions and garlic, sauté until golden brown.
- Add the lobster meat and flambé with the brandy, add the mushrooms and simmer for a few minutes, stir in the mustard, Tabasco and Worcestershire and cook over low flame a few more minutes.
- Mix in the white sauce, remove from fire and add the parsley. Season with salt and pepper and fill the shells with the mixture, sprinkle with the breadcrumbs and place under the broiler for a few minutes to glaze.
- Let it cool for a few minutes then gradually add some hot fish stock, whisk continuously to prevent lumps. Bring the mixture slowly to boil and let simmer for 15 to 20 minutes.
- WHITE SAUCE: In a saucepan, melt equal parts of butter and flour (over low heat), whisk them together (do not let the mixture get brown) until you obtain a homogenous paste. Let it cool for a few minutes and then gradually add hot fish stock, whisking continuously to prevent lumps. Bring the mixture slowly to a boil and let simmer for 15 to 20 minutes.

Caribbean Chicken

Ingredients

- 3 broiler-fryers chicken; (about 2 lb each), cut in half
- salt and pepper to taste
- 1 cup butter or margarine
- ⅓ cup lemon or lime juice
- 1 TB Italian seasoning, crushed
- 2 ½ tsp salt
- 2 garlic cloves, crushed
- ¾ tsp dry mustard
- ¼ tsp coarse black pepper
- 1 ½ cups orange marmalade
- 3 TB lemon or lime juice
- 3 TB butter or margarine

Preparation

- In a small saucepan, melt 1 cup butter over low heat, stir in 1/3 cup lemon or lime juice, Italian seasoning, 2-1/2 teaspoons salt, garlic, dry mustard and 1/4 teaspoon pepper.
- Sprinkle each side of chicken halves lightly with salt and pepper. Place chicken on grill skin side up; brush with herb butter.
- Grill about 4 to 5 inches from medium coals until chicken is tender, about 1 hour. Baste frequently, turn chicken occasionally.
- Meanwhile, combine marmalade with 3 tablespoons lemon or lime juice and 3 tablespoons butter in saucepan.
- Heat, stirring constantly, until melted. About 4 minutes before chicken is done, brush some of the marmalade mixture on each chicken half to glaze; grill about 1 minute.
- Turn chicken; brush with remaining marmalade mixture; grill about 1 more minute. Makes 6 servings.

Caribbean Salad Platter

Ingredients

- 3 cups watercress
- 3 large mangoes, pitted, peeled and cut into chunks
- 2 14 oz. cans of hearts of palm, drained, rinsed and sliced
- 2 large tomatoes, cut into large chunks
- ⅓ cup lime juice
- ¼ tsp coriander
- ¼ tsp allspice
- lime wedges for garnish

Preparation

- Arrange watercress around the perimeter of a large platter. Arrange alternating rows of mango, hearts of palm & tomatoes to fill platter.
- Combine lime juice, coriander & allspice in a small bowl. Cover & refrigerate at least 30 minutes before serving. Serve with extra lime wedges if desired.

Jamaican Beef Patties

Ingredients

- 4 cups all-purpose flour
- 1 tsp salt

- 1 ¼ cups shortening
- 6 To 8 TB ice water

FILLING
- 1 large onion, finely diced
- 4 garlic cloves, minced
- 3 jalapenos, seeded, stemmed and minced
- 3 TB vegetable oil
- ¾ lb ground beef
- 2 tsp each of ground coriander, cumin, and turmeric
- 1 tsp each of ground allspice and cinnamon
- 1 green bell pepper, stemmed, seeded and finely chopped
- 4 tomatoes, minced
- 1 bunch green onions, minced
- salt and pepper to taste
- 2 eggs, lightly beaten

Preparation

- Pastry: Preheat the oven to 400 deg F. To make the dough: place the flour and salt in a large bowl; mix well. Cut the shortening into small pieces about the size of walnuts.
- Add to the flour and, using your fingers, rub the flour and shortening together, making coarse, mealy dough. Add the ice water and gather the dough into a ball.
- The dough should be firm and not sticky. If the dough is too dry, add a little more water, but if the dough is too sticky, add just enough flour to make it form a ball.
- Divide the dough into 2 equal balls and cover with plastic wrap. Refrigerate for at least 2 hours or up to 2 days.
- To make the filling: in a large skillet, cook the onion, garlic, and chilies in the oil over moderate heat for about 10 minutes, stirring from time to time.
- Add the beef, herbs, spices, bell pepper, and tomatoes, and cook over high heat for 5 minutes, stirring constantly until the mixture is thick and saucy. Add the green onions and cook for 1 minute.
- Season with salt and pepper and cool to room temperature. To assemble the patties: on a lightly floured surface, divide each ball into 2 equal balls, so that you have 4 equal balls.
- Flatten into disc shapes, then divide each disc into 6 equal pieces and roll each into a ball. Roll each ball into a 3 1/2 inch diameter circle.
- Brush the edges with beaten egg. Place about 1 tablespoon of filling on one side of each circle, leaving a 1/4 inch border.
- Fold the dough over, making a half-moon shape. Seal the edges with the tines of a fork, and brush with the remaining egg.
- Bake on a lightly greased baking sheet for 25 to 30 minutes, or until the

patties are golden brown. Remove from the oven and serve immediately.

Jamaican Oxtails

Ingredients
- 3 lb oxtails, trimmed
- 1 onion, sliced
- ¼ cup soy sauce
- ¼ cup flour
- ½ tsp salt
- 1 tsp pepper
- ¼ cup oil
- 1 tomato, chopped
- 1 bell pepper, chopped
- 1 habanero chile, chopped (HOT!)
- 1 clove garlic, pressed
- 6 cups hot water
- 3 TB molasses
- 1 thyme sprig

Preparation
- Place oxtails in a large bowl. Add sliced onion and soy sauce. Mix well. Refrigerate at least 2 hours.
- Combine flour, salt and pepper. Dredge oxtails in mixture making sure all sides are covered. Reserve onion. Heat oil in large Dutch oven until hot. Brown oxtails.
- Remove meat from pan; drain off all but 1-2 tablespoons oil. Add reserved onion, tomato, bell pepper, chile and garlic to pan and sauté lightly, scraping up brown bits.
- Add hot water and molasses and stir well. Return oxtails to pan and cook over low heat for 1-1/2 hours. Add thyme sprig and continue to cook 30 minutes longer.

Paella Panamanian Style

Ingredients
- 3 lb chicken, cut up
- 4 pork chops, cut into small cubes
- 2 lobsters
- 1 lb squid, sliced
- 1 ½ lb small shrimp

- 3 lb small clams, sliced
- 2 lb pork sausage, cut into small pieces
- 2 lb sausage, Spanish or Italian
- 1/2 lb razor clams or longorones
- 4 large onions, minced
- 4 green peppers, minced
- 5 garlic cloves, minced
- 3 fresh tomatoes or 1 can of tomatoes
- 1 can tomato paste
- 1 can tomato sauce
- 1 can chick peas
- salt to taste
- pepper to taste
- parsley to taste
- scallions to taste
- 6 TB oil
- 5 cups rice
- ½ jar stuffed olives

Preparation

- Cut and fry the chicken well. Make a sauce with 1 ½ onions, 1 1/2 green pepper, 1 1/2 tomatoes, cut up, and 3 cloves of garlic.
- Add 1 cup water and chicken. Cook on a low heat. Separately fry the sausage in small pieces and the pork chops. Boil the lobsters and shrimp and peel them.
- Clean and slice clams and squid. Make a sauce with 1 1/2 onion, 1 1/2 green pepper, 1 1/2 tomatoes and the liquid from the Chick Peas.
- Separate the meat from the bones of all meats and cook the clams with the scallions and parsley.
- Make sauce with the remaining onion, scallion, finely chopped green pepper, tomato paste and tomato sauce. Wash the rice well (3 times) and in a large, deep pot, put 6 tablespoons oil and fry the rice.
- Add the liquid the seafood was cooked in (about 5 cups). Add sausage, boneless chicken and pork with their sauces, whole shrimp, lobster sliced into small pieces, clam and squid and mussels in their sauce.
- Also, add the sauce made with the remaining onion, scallion, finely chopped green pepper, tomato paste and tomato sauce. Add the Chick peas and olives.
- Cook at a high heat for 10 minutes; then cover pot and cook at a low heat for 45 minutes. When ready to serve, decorate with strips of green peppers and olives.

Pork Chops With Bananas and Bacon

Ingredients
- 4 pork chops, 1 inch thick
- ¾ TB cumin
- salt and pepper to taste
- 1 lemon, juiced
- 2 TB butter; softened
- 2 large bananas
- 6 strips bacon,
- Beer (opt)

Preparation
- Combine the butter, salt, pepper and cumin. Rub into both sides of the meat. Sauté the bacon briefly, until some of the fat has rendered.
- Remove and drain. Peel bananas and cut into 1 ¼ inch chunks. Place on a dish and sprinkle with lemon juice.
- Slice the bacon in strips long enough to wrap around each banana slice. Place on skewers, threading through the bacon. Place the pork chops on a hot grill, for 15 minutes, turning once.
- Turn grill down to medium, adding the bacon and bananas; grill another 10 minutes, turning both the meat and bananas. Also good basted with beer, while the meat cooks.

Huevos Habaneros
(Eggs Havana Style)

Ingredients
SAUCE
- ¼ cup pure Spanish olive oil
- 1 small onion, finely chopped
- 1 small green bell pepper, finely chopped
- 2 cloves garlic, finely chopped
- 1 cup canned tomatoes, drained and chopped or prepared tomato sauce
- ½ cup pimento, drained and finely chopped
- 2 TB dry sherry
- salt to taste
- fresh ground black pepper to taste

EGGS

- 8 large eggs
- 4 TB salted butter
- Salt and fresh ground pepper to taste
- 1 TB chopped parsley, finely chopped for garnish

Preparation

- Preheat oven to 350 degrees. In a medium-size skillet over low heat, heat the oil until it is fragrant, and then cook the onion, bell pepper, and garlic, stirring, until tender, 8 to 10 minutes.
- Add the tomatoes, pimientos, and sherry, cook until thickened, 15 minutes, and season with salt and pepper.
- Lightly oil 4 ramekins or au gratin dishes and divide the sauce among them. For each dish, break two eggs into a saucer, slide them on top of the tomato mixture, and drizzle with 1 tablespoon melted butter.
- Bake until the whites are set and the yolks are still soft, 10 to 12 minutes. Sprinkle with salt, pepper, and parsley, and serve immediately from the baking dishes. (Place each on a serving plate, to protect the table).

Caribbean Banana Dessert

Ingredients

- 1 TB lemon peel
- 1 TB orange peel
- 1 TB lemon juice
- 3 TB orange juice
- 3 cups banana chunks
- 3 tsp egg replacer (powdered eggs) mixed with 4 TB water
- ⅓ cup brown sugar
- 3 TB pineapple juice
- 1 cup soy milk
- 1 cup breadcrumbs
- 2 TB soy margarine, melted and cooled

Preparation

- Preheat oven to 300F. Oil a 1 1/2 quart mould. Combine peels & juices with banana & set aside.
- Place egg replacer, sugar & pineapple juice in a food processor & pulse till blended. Add soy milk & bread crumbs & pulse a few more times. Spoon mixture over banana mixture.
- Add margarine, mix well & pour into prepared mold. Place mold in a large pan & pour in enough boiling water to reach halfway up the sides of the mould.

- Bake 1 hour 20 minutes, a knife inserted should come out clean. You may have to add more boiling water during the cooking time.
- Cool 20 to 30 minutes & then remove from the mould. Refrigerate 2 hours before serving.

Caribbean Grouper
With Mango, Pear and Avocado Salad

Ingredients
- 3 lbs black grouper fillet, skin on
- 4 mangoes, sliced in ¼ inch strips
- 6 red pears, sliced in ¼ inch strips
- ½ pound cleaned baby spinach
- 3 Haas avocados, sliced in ¼ inch strips
- walnut oil
- juice of two oranges
- juice of one lime

CARIBBEAN SEASONING
- 6 TB minced garlic
- 6 TB minced onion
- 6 TB dried onion
- 2 TB allspice
- 1 TB chipotle
- 2 TB Hungarian paprika
- 2 TB brown sugar
- 4 ½ tsp thyme
- 4 ½ tsp cinnamon
- 1 ½ tsp nutmeg
- ½ tsp ground habanero
- zest of two lemons

Preparation
- Prepare a wood or charcoal grill and let it burn down to embers. Rub on the Caribbean seasoning in long strokes. Let sit for 15 minutes.
- Grill for 8 minutes on one side and 6 minutes on the reverse side. Remove from grill and keep hot.
- Lightly oil the fruit with walnut oil and grill over hickory wood for 3 minutes. Place in a bowl with the fruit juices and toss. Serve on top of baby spinach and avocado.

Crabs Caribbean Style

Ingredients
- 8 TB butter
- 4 scallions, chopped
- 1-2 tsp garlic, chopped
- 1 hot green chili, finely chopped and seeded (or use dried red pepper-flakes)
- 1 TB curry powder
- ¾ - 1 lb crab meat, shredded
- 2 TB fresh coriander leaves, chopped
- 2 TB parsley, finely chopped
- salt and freshly ground pepper
- 6 – 8 TB crab liquid or clam broth
- 2 cups bread crumbs

Preparation
- Melt butter in skillet; add scallions, garlic and chili peppers and cook until scallions are wilted. Add curry powder to this mixture and blend thoroughly.
- Add crab, coriander and parsley. Add salt, pepper and crab liquid (if more is needed, add melted butter). Blend in bread crumbs.
- Fill the mixture in 8 clam shells and bake at 400 degrees F about 10 minutes or until browned. Serves 8 as an appetizer or 3 to 4 as a main course.

Curry Mutton or Goat

Ingredients
- 2 lbs mutton
- 3 onions
- 1 bunch herbs
- 1 clove garlic
- 1 tsp salt
- ½ lb carrots
- 2 TB curry powder
- 1 tsp sugar
- 2 TB tomato ketchup
- 1 TB fat

Preparation
- Cut meat in pieces, fry lightly in fat, add curry powder and simmer in water to cover with seasonings until meat is nearly tender (1 1/2 hours)
- Dice carrots and add. Continue cooking until meat and carrots are tender.

Caribbean Seafood Chowder

Ingredients
- 2 lb assorted firm-fleshed fish, snapper, drum, trout (reserve fish bones)
- 1 lb large shrimp, peeled and deveined (reserve shrimp shells)
- ⅓ cup fresh lime juice
- 2 jalapeno chilies, seeded and minced
- 2 onions, divided
- 4 cloves garlic, divided
- 3 stalks celery, divided
- 6 cups cold water
- ⅓ cup thick-sliced bacon, diced
- 2 sweet peppers, seeded and finely chopped
- 3 cups potatoes, diced
- ½ tsp dried thyme
- 2 bay leaves
- ¼ tsp nutmeg, freshly grated
- 4 cups tomatoes, peeled and chopped
- ¼ cup tomato paste (optional)
- beer
- cayenne and black pepper, to taste

Preparation
- Cut fish in 2-inch cubes. Toss together fish, shrimp, lime juice, and jalapenos. Refrigerate for 2 hours.
- Place fish bones and shrimp shells in stockpot with one unpeeled onion, one unpeeled garlic clove -both quartered- and one celery rib.
- Cover with water and simmer one hour. Drain and discard solids. Reserve stock. Sauté bacon until browned. Reserve bacon.
- Sauté remaining three onions, two celery ribs, and both peppers until tender and golden.
- Add garlic, finely minced, and sauté a minute longer. Add potatoes, thyme bay and nutmeg; cover with hot stock, tomatoes and tomato paste (if used).
- Cook until potatoes are barely tender, about 15 to 20 minutes. Add fish and shrimp along with their marinade.
- Simmer another 10 to 15 minutes until done. Thin with beer, if needed,

and adjust heat level to suit you.

Jerk Chicken
With Pineapple Salsa Jambalaya

Ingredients
- 1 cup couscous
- 1 TB vegetable oil
- 4 boneless skinless chicken breasts
- salt
- freshly ground black pepper
- ½ cup chicken broth
- 2 TB Jamaican jerk sauce
- 3 green onions, sliced

SALSA
- 8 oz pineapple, fresh cut
- 1 red pepper, diced
- ½ cup mango chutney
- ¼ cup fresh cilantro, chopped

Preparation
- Cook couscous according to package directions. Meanwhile, heat oil in a large skillet over medium-high heat.
- Sprinkle both sides of chicken with salt and pepper. Add to skillet and cook until firm, 4 to 5 minutes per side. Transfer cooked chicken to serving plate; keep warm.
- Add chicken broth and jerk sauce to skillet and bring to boil; boil 1 minute. Pour over chicken. Sprinkle with green onions.
- Serve with couscous, Pineapple Salsa and lime wedges. PINEAPPLE SALSA: While chicken is cooking, combine pineapple, red pepper, chutney and cilantro in bowl. Stir to combine. Makes 4 cups.

Trinidad Congo Pepper Salsa

Ingredients
- 15 habanero peppers (or scotch bonnet), stemmed, seeded and minced
- 2 large white onions, minced
- 1 papaya, peeled and diced
- 1 mango, peeled, pitted and diced
- 2 TB Dijon mustard

- ½ tsp turmeric
- ½ tsp curry powder
- 3 cups vinegar

Preparation

- Place all ingredients in a pan, bring to boil, lower the heat, and let simmer for 30 minutes.
- Remove from heat, cool, and store in a jar in refrigerator.

###

Part 4: French Recipes

French cuisine *offers a rich experience that ranges from simple, rustic country dishes to elaborate gastronomic feats. Based in a complex history of cultural influences and a wide array of ingredients, it is limited only by the imagination of the cook preparing it. With basic cooking techniques and a little practice, you can begin enjoying authentic French cuisine in your own kitchen in no time!*

Brioches

Ingredients
- 2 ¼ cups sifted flour
- ½ cup milk, heated to lukewarm (105F)
- 1 pack active dry yeast
- 1 TB sugar
- 3 egg yolks
- 1 whole egg
- 6 TB butter, melted and cooled

Preparation
- Place flour in a large mixing bowl. Make a well in the center and pour in the milk.
- Sprinkle yeast and sugar over milk, stir, and let stand until foamy (about 5 minutes).
- With two spoons, stir together liquid and dry ingredients. Cover with a tea towel and let stand in a warm place until mixture bubbles and rises slightly (about 25 minutes).
- Mix in egg yolks and butter. Add lukewarm milk, a little at a time, until workable dough is formed.
- With a wooden spoon, work dough until smooth and shiny (5-10 minutes). Cover with a tea towel and set in a warm place to rise until double (1 – 1 1/2 hours).
- Preheat oven to 400 degrees. Punch down dough.
- With a teaspoon, scoop out pieces of dough about the size of an egg and form them into balls. Place the balls well-spaced on an ungreased baking sheet.
- Crack the whole egg into a small bowl and beat well; brush egg on top of dough balls.
- Let stand in warm place 15-20 minutes and then brush with egg again.
- Place in oven and immediately reduce temperature to 375F. Bake until golden (20-25 minutes). Let cool on wire rack.

Chocolate Mint Mousse

Ingredients
- 8 oz semisweet chocolate
- 4 egg yolks
- ⅓ cup granulated sugar
- ⅓ cup white crème de menthe
- 1 ½ tsp unflavored gelatin (1/2 package)
- 2 cups heavy cream
- fresh mint sprigs for garnish (optional)

Preparation
- Chop the chocolate into small pieces and put into a bowl. In a medium saucepan, bring 2 inches of water to a simmer. Remove pan from heat. Set the bowl of chocolate over the hot water, stirring frequently until just melted. Remove bowl from hot water. Cool.
- Bring the water in the saucepan back to a simmer. In a large bowl or in the bowl of a standing mixer, combine the egg yolks, sugar, and crème de menthe. Set bowl over simmering water and whisk constantly until egg mixture is slightly thickened, about 3 minutes. Remove bowl from hot water.
- With mixer on medium speed, whisk the egg mixture until light and cool, about 4 minutes. In a small saucepan, bring about 1 inch of water to a simmer. Put 1/4 cup of water in a small bowl, sprinkle with gelatin, and let stand until softened, about 2 minutes.
- Remove pan of simmering water from heat and set bowl of softened gelatin in hot water until gelatin has melted, about 2 minutes. Whip cream to soft peaks. Whisk gelatin into cool egg mixture, and then divide egg-gelatin mixture evenly between two bowls. Fold 1/2 of the whipped cream into one of the bowls.
- Stir melted chocolate into second bowl and then fold in remaining whipped cream. To layer the mousse, divide 1/2 of the Chocolate Mint Mouse between six individual goblets.
- Spoon all of the mint mousse on top. Make a final layer using the remaining Chocolate Mint Mousse. Refrigerate until set, at least 2 hours. Recipe can be prepared and refrigerated 1 day ahead. Serves 6.

Creamy Chestnut Soup

Ingredients

- 4 lb peeled chestnuts, fresh-whole (8 cups)
- 1 medium onion
- 12 medium shallots
- 4 stalks celery
- 5 oz prosciutto, sliced
- 3 TB butter
- 2 ½ qt unsalted chicken stock
- 1 tsp fennel seeds
- 1 bay leaf
- ½ tsp salt
- ½ cup heavy cream
- ½ tsp fresh ground white pepper
- ¼ cup cèpes (or porcini) mushrooms, dried

Preparation

- Adjust oven rack to middle position and heat oven to 400F. With a small, sharp knife, slit the outer shell of each chestnut, put them in a shallow baking pan, and roast until tender, 15 to 20 minutes.
- Peel off the outer shells and inner skins while still warm. Reheat if the chestnuts cool and become difficult to peel. Peel and thinly slice the onion and the shallots. Thinly slice the celery tops and leaves (reserve ribs for another use).
- Julienne the prosciutto. Wrap and refrigerate 2 tablespoons prosciutto for garnish.
- COOKING: Heat 2 tablespoons of the butter in an 8-quart soup kettle and sauté the onion, shallots and remaining prosciutto over medium heat until softened, about 5 minutes.
- In a large saucepan, bring 6 cups of the chicken stock to a boil. Stir the hot chicken stock into the shallot mixture along with the chestnuts, celery, fennel seeds, bay leaf, and 1/2 teaspoon salt.
- Bring the mixture to a boil and skim. Reduce the heat and simmer, covered, for 45 minutes. Remove and set aside 16 chestnuts for garnish. Continue simmering until remaining chestnuts are very tender, about 45 minutes longer.
- Remove soup from heat, discard the bay leaf, and set aside to cool 15 minutes. Pour the soup into the work bowl of a food processor fitted with a metal blade, or into a blender.
- Pure, then strain through a fine sieve or tamis. (Can cover and refrigerate up to 3 days, or freeze up to 1 month.) Serves 8.

Croutons

Ingredients
- ⅓ cup butter
- 3 cloves garlic, finely minced
- 2 cup bread cubes
- salt
- black pepper

Preparation
- Heat oven to 400F. Lightly brown the diced garlic in the butter. Add cubed bread. (It works better if it is a little old, but if you only have fresh, just be more gentle).
- Toss well, but gently to coat the bread with the butter. Set in oven and roast for about 7 minutes, then stir well and roast again for about 7 minutes more. When bread has taken on a golden color, remove and salt and pepper to taste.
- Spread out on a large platter to cool. Bread will become crunchy as it sits. Yields: 2 cups

Herb Pâté

Ingredients
- 1 lb pork with fat
- 1//2 lb boneless veal
- 1 large onion, chopped
- 3 cloves garlic, minced
- 1 TB butter
- 1 ½ cups spinach, spinach
- 3 TB brandy
- 1 egg
- 1 ½ TB fresh basil
- 1 ½ TB fresh rosemary
- 1 TB fresh thyme
- 1 ½ tsp salt
- 1 ½ tsp fennel seeds
- ¾ tsp black pepper
- 6 slices bacon
- 3 hardboiled eggs

Preparation

- Preheat oven to 350F. In a food processor or meat grinder, grind pork and veal fine. In a frying pan, sauté onion and garlic in butter. Add spinach; cook minute. Transfer spinach mixture to a large bowl and stir in chopped meat.
- Add brandy, egg, and all herbs and spices. Fry a patty and adjust seasoning. Arrange bacon across bottom and sides of an 8 1/2- by 4 1/2-inch loaf pan, letting slices hang over edges.
- Put half the meat mixture into pan. Put hard-cooked eggs, lengthwise, down center of meat. Add remaining meat mixture and wrap bacon across top. Cover pan with foil, set in a baking pan, and add water to come halfway up the pt.
- Bring to a simmer and then put into oven and bake until a skewer inserted into the center for 1/2 minute is very hot when withdrawn, about 1 1/4 hours.
- Remove from oven and let stand, uncovered, for 30 minutes. Cover and weight evenly. Refrigerate 24 hours. To serve, remove from pan and trim fat. Bring to room temperature.

Herbed Brown Butter

Ingredients

- 5 TB butter (or clarified butter)
- 1 tsp lemon juice, lime juice or vinegar
- 1 TB chopped chives, dill, parsley or any combination
- Black pepper

Preparation

- This is really best if you can take the time to clarify the butter: heat it just to the melting point, let stand a few minutes, skim the whey and drain off the fat to use.
- Discard the whey. Brown the butter over low heat. Stir and cook until it turns dark brown. Stir in the lemon juice or vinegar and the herbs of choice, then pepper to taste. Yields: 5 tablespoons

Home Made French Dressing

Ingredients
- 1 cup oil
- 1 cup vinegar
- 1 tsp dry mustard
- 1 small onion, finely chopped
- ½ cup ketchup
- ½ cup sugar
- 1 tsp salt (optional)

Preparation
- Mix all together in a glass quart bottle that has a tight fitting lid. Store in the fridge. Keeps for weeks and weeks!!

Leeks Vinaigrette
(Poireaux En Salade)

Ingredients
- 12 leeks
- ¼ cup olive oil
- 4 tsp vinegar
- salt
- fresh ground black pepper
- 1 TB fresh parsley, chopped
- mustard, to taste

Preparation
- Clean the leeks; cut off most of the green parts and wash leeks very thoroughly, split if necessary, under cold running water.
- If they are large, do split them lengthwise; each piece should be about the size of a large stalk of asparagus. Tie them into bundles in two places, put them in boiling salted water just to cover, and cook them slowly for 25 minutes, or until they are tender but not limp.
- Drain them well (and be sure to save the broth to add to a soup). The leeks may be presented in a serving dish or arranged on individual plates.
- Make your vinaigrette in a bowl, adding mustard to taste, and whisk the dressing well until it is almost opaque, or emulsified, and pour it over the leeks. Serves: 3 to 4

Madeira Cream Sauce

Ingredients
- 2 Shallots
- 1 TB butter
- ¼ cup dry white wine
- ¼ cup Madeira
- 1 cup heavy cream
- salt
- black pepper, fresh ground

Preparation
- Mince the shallots. Melt the butter in medium saucepan over low heat. Add the shallots and sauté until soft, about 2 minutes.
- Add the white wine, bring to a boil, and cook until reduced to 2 tablespoons, about 3 minutes. Add the Madeira and bring to a boil. Stir in the cream and bring to a boil.
- Reduce heat to medium and simmer, stirring frequently, until sauce is thick enough to coat the back of a spoon, about 5 minutes. Season to taste with salt and pepper. Yields: 1 1/2 cups

Parfait Tort

Ingredients
- 6 oz ladyfinger cookies
- 1 ½ cups milk
- ½ cup rum
- ⅔ cup sugar
- 4 eggs yolks
- 2 TB flour
- 1 tsp vanilla extract
- ½ cup butter, softened
- ¾ cup almonds or walnuts, coarsely ground
- 1 cup whipping cream, for topping
- candied fruit, for garnish

Preparation
- Line the bottom and sides of a 9-inch spring form pan with about half of the ladyfingers. In a small bowl mix together-cup of the milk and 1/4 cup of the rum; sprinkle over ladyfingers.
- In the top pan of a double boiler, combine the remaining milk, 1/3 cup of

- the sugar, egg yolks, flour, and vanilla. Place over gently boiling water and cook, stirring constantly, until mixture is thickened and coats the back of a spoon.
- Remove from heat and let cool. In a medium bowl cream together butter and the remaining sugar until smooth. Add cooled egg-yolk mixture and nuts; beat until fluffy. Gradually add the remaining rum, beating constantly.
- Pour creamed mixture over ladyfinger-lined pan, being careful not to dislodge ladyfingers. Arrange remaining ladyfingers over filling. Cover torte and refrigerate overnight.
- When ready to serve, remove pan sides. Whip cream until stiff peaks form and spoon attractively on top of torte.

Potato-Onion Soup with Arugula

Ingredients
- 1 medium onion, roughly chopped
- 2 TB butter
- ½ tsp salt
- 4 medium potatoes, peeled and cubed
- 1 qt chicken stock
- 1 cup arugula, chopped
- ½ cup cream
- extra virgin olive oil (optional)
- black pepper

Preparation
- Melt the butter in a soup pot and soften the onion with the salt over medium heat for about five minutes (don't brown).
- Add the potatoes, stir briefly, then add the chicken stock, bring to a boil and simmer until the potatoes are tender, about 15 minutes. Stir in the arugula, return to a boil, add the cream, and then remove from the heat when it just comes back to the boil.
- Serve with a teaspoon or two of olive oil and a good grinding of pepper in each bowl.

Provençale Stuffing

Ingredients

- 1 TB olive oil
- ¾ cup onion, chopped
- 2 large cloves garlic, minced
- 1 large tomato, peeled and coarsely chopped
- 2 ½ TB fresh parsley, chopped
- 2 tsp fresh basil, chopped
- 1 ½ tsp fresh thyme, chopped
- ½ tsp salt
- ¼ tsp black pepper
- ¾ cup bread crumbs
- ¼ cup parmesan cheese

Preparation

- Peel tomato and coarsely chop. Set aside. Heat skillet with oil to medium heat and sauté onion and garlic for about 2 minutes. Stir in tomato, herbs and seasonings. Sauté for about 4 minutes or until wetness evaporates.
- Remove from heat and stir in breadcrumbs and Parmesan cheese. Stuff parboiled cabbage leaves, whole tomatoes that have had the pulp scooped out, or zucchini or eggplant that has been half-baked.
- Top with more Parmesan cheese and bake for 15 to 30 minutes depending on the size and quantity of the stuffed vegetable. Yields: 1 cup

Quiche Lorraine

Ingredients

- 1 pie crust
- 12 slices bacon, fried, drained and crumbled
- 1 ½ cup Swiss cheese, grated

MIX TOGETHER

- 5 Eggs
- 2 cups light cream (or milk)
- ¼ tsp paprika
- ½ tsp salt
- ⅛ tsp white pepper
- ⅛ tsp nutmeg

Preparation

- Heat the oven to 400F. Prepare the pie shell, sprinkle half of the Swiss cheese in the shell then crumble the fried bacon over the cheese. Sprinkle remaining cheese evenly over the bacon.

- Mix together egg mixture until well-blended and pour slowly over the bacon and cheese, taking care not to create bare spots. Cover pie crust edges with a thin strip of foil and bake quiche at 400F for 15 minutes.
- Reduce heat to 350F and bake for 20 minutes more. Remove foil covering and bake 10 minutes more. Serve like pie. Yields: 1 9-inch pie

Sautéed Lamb Medallions
(With Red Wine and Fresh Mint)

Ingredients
- 1 ½ lb saddle of lamb, split, with loins barded and (1 ½ to 2 lbs) aprons
- 1 medium onion
- 1 medium carrot
- 2 cloves garlic
- 1 leek
- 3 TB vegetable oil
- ½ cup fresh mint, loosely packed leaves
- ½ tsp dried thyme
- 1 bay leaf
- 2 cups fresh lamb (or beef) stock, or canned beef broth
- 1 ½ cup red Bordeaux wine such as merlot (or cabernet)
- 2 TB butter, chilled

Preparation
- Trim the apron meat of all fat and set aside. Peel the onion, carrot, and garlic. Coarsely chop the onion and carrot, and set aside with the garlic in a small bowl.
- Trim, clean, and coarsely chop the leek (using all of the white section and about 2 inches of the green tops), and add it to the bowl. In a heavy, medium, non-reactive skillet, heat 1 tablespoon of the oil.
- Quarter each apron and sauté over medium heat until very brown, about 7 minutes. Measure 2 tablespoons mint leaves (wrap and refrigerate the remaining mint and add to the skillet along with the chopped vegetables, thyme, and bay leaf.
- Cover the skillet, lower the heat, and cook, stirring occasionally, until the vegetables are lightly colored and tender, about 20 minutes. Stir in the lamb stock and red wine and bring to a boil.
- Lower the heat and simmer, partially covered, skimming frequently, until strained liquid reduces to 1 1/4 cups, about 50-60 minutes. Discard solids and set strained liquid aside. (Can cover and refrigerate up to 2 days.)

- Mince the remaining mint leaves. Cut the butter into small pieces and set aside. Slice loins into six to eight 1-1/4-inch thick medallions and sprinkle with salt and pepper. In a large, heavy, non-reactive skillet, heat the remaining 2 tablespoons oil until very hot, but not smoking.
- Sauté medallions 2 minutes on each side until medium rare. Transfer medallions to a plate and cover loosely with foil to keep warm. Increase heat to high, pour the strained stock into the skillet and bring to a boil, scraping the bottom of the skillet with a wooden spoon to deglaze.
- Boil until stock reduces to 1 cup, 2-3 minutes. Remove skillet from heat and whisk in butter, one piece at a time. Stir in the mint and season to taste with salt and pepper. Cover and keep sauce warm.
- Transfer medallions to a cutting board and stir accumulated juices into the sauce. Remove string (and barding, if used) and put medallions onto individual plates. Spoon sauce around medallions; serve immediately.

Savory Butter

Ingredients
- 2 TB summer savory leaves, stems removed
- 6 TB butter, softened

Preparation
- Mince the summer savory, then cream the butter, and beat in the savory. Shape the herb butter into a 1-inch-thick cylinder, wrap in plastic, and refrigerate. Yields: 3/4 cup

Smoked Fish Pâté Canapés

Ingredients
- Scallions
- ¾ lb smoked cod or trout, boneless and skinless
- ¼ lb butter, softened
- ¼ lb cream cheese, softened
- 3 TB fresh dill
- 1 TB horseradish
- 2 TB sour cream
- salt
- black pepper
- 1 TB lemon juice

- 2 cucumbers
- ½ loaf rye bread
- 12 radishes
- dill for garnish

Preparation

- For the pate, chop scallions. Combine the trout, butter, and cream cheese in the bowl of a food processor and process for a few seconds. Add the scallions, dill, and horseradish and process until just smooth with bits of herbs still visible.
- Briefly pulse in sour cream. Season with salt, pepper, and 1 tablespoon lemon juice. Refrigerate for at least 4 hours. Pate can be made a few days ahead. Slice cucumbers into 3/16-inch- thick rounds.
- Cut radishes into paper-thin slices. Fill a pastry bag fitted with a 1/2-inch star tip with pate. Pipe generous rosettes on top of each cucumber slice. Garnish with radish slices and dill.
- As an alternative, toast bread and cut into ovals with a pastry cutter or into rectangles or squares with a knife. Pipe pt onto bread and garnish with radishes and fresh dill.
- Put in jelly roll pans or baking pans, cover well, and refrigerate. Canapés can be made a few hours ahead.

Spring Vegetable Blanquette

Ingredients

- 12 pearl onions, about 3 ounces
- 8 asparagus spears, about ½ lb
- salt
- 12 baby carrots, about ¼ lb
- 3 ounces mushrooms, chopped small, about ¾ cup
- ¾ lb fresh peas, shelled or frozen peas, thawed
- 1 cup chicken stock
- ½ cup heavy cream
- 1 TB fresh tarragon leaves, minced
- 1 TB fresh chives, minced
- 1 TB fresh parsley, minced
- 1 tsp lemon juice
- fresh ground black pepper

Preparation

- Put unpeeled onions in a small saucepan with enough water to cover, bring to a boil, and cook for 1 minute. Drain, rinse under cold water, and drain

again. Peel onions. Trim and peel asparagus stalks, cut off tips, and cut stalks into 1-inch lengths.
- Cook asparagus in 2 quarts of boiling, salted water for 2 minutes. Drain and refresh under cold water. Trim carrots, cutting any large ones in half crosswise. Quarter the mushrooms. Shell the peas.
- Bring stock and 1/2 cup water to a boil in a medium saucepan. Add the carrots, cover, and simmer over medium heat until just tender, about 12 minutes. With a slotted spoon, remove carrots from the pan and put in a large bowl.
- Add mushrooms and onions to pan, cover, and simmer until onions are just tender, about 10 minutes. Transfer mushrooms and onions to the bowl. Add the peas to the saucepan, bring to a boil, and cook, uncovered, just until tender, about 4 minutes. (Cook 1 minute if using frozen peas.)
- Transfer peas to the bowl, and drain any liquid from the bowl into the saucepan. Bring vegetable cooking liquid to a boil and cook until reduced to ¼ cup, about 5 minutes.
- Whisk cream into cooking liquid, bring to a boil and cook, whisking often, until sauce is thick enough to coat the back of a spoon, about 4 minutes. Remove pan from heat. Recipe can be made to this point a few hours ahead.
- Cool and cover sauce with plastic wrap touching its surface; set sauce aside at room temperature. Bring sauce to a simmer in a large saucepan. Add vegetables to pan and simmer over medium heat, stirring gently, until just warmed through, about 2 minutes.
- Remove pan from heat. Add the tarragon, chives, parsley, and lemon juice. Toss gently, season to taste with salt and pepper.

Coq Au Vin
(Simplified)

Ingredients
- 1 cut up chicken, dredged in flour
- ¼ lb bacon, minced
- 1 medium onion, chopped
- 1 medium carrot, thinly sliced
- 1 clove garlic, peeled and minced
- ½ lb mushrooms, sliced
- 1 bay leaf
- ½ tsp thyme
- salt and pepper to taste
- 1 TB marjoram
- 1 1/2 cups dry red wine (or to taste)

- 2-4 drops Kitchen Bouquet

Preparation
- In a heavy, deep skillet or Dutch oven, cook bacon until firm. Retaining bacon fat, add all vegetables except mushrooms and cook until browned.
- Add mushrooms and cook until limp. Remove vegetables, set aside, and brown chicken pieces in remaining fat. Add red wine and herbs and reserved vegetables.
- Simmer, covered for 45 minutes to an hour, turning once. Just before serving add Kitchen Bouquet.

Chocolate Truffles

Ingredients
- 1 cup heavy cream
- 10 oz bittersweet chocolate, chopped
- 3 TB sweet butter
- 1- 1 ½ lb bittersweet chocolate
- 6 oz almonds, blanched, cooled and skins removed (optional)

Preparation
- In a heavy pan, bring the cream to a simmer (a microwave and a glass bowl is just as good for this). Remove from the heat and whisk in the chocolate and butter. (The smaller they are cut up, the easier this will be.)
- Refrigerate until firmly set, stirring now and then. In the refrigerator compartment this will take about 4 hours. Use the freezer and you can cut that down to under an hour, but with much more frequent stirring.
- Using a melon baller or spoon, scoop out a tablespoon or so of chocolate and use your hands to form balls about 3/4" to 1" in diameter. Spread them on a cookie sheet and freeze for an hour.
- While the balls are freezing, chop and carefully heat, in a double boiler or heavy pot, the remaining chocolate. Stir until melted. Allow to slowly cool until it feels just warm to your skin.
- The object is to have it just above the melting point so that when the frozen chocolate balls are dipped in it, they gather and congeal a thick coating around them.
- When the centers are frozen and the chocolate is ready, take each one and drop it into the coating, roll it quickly about, then remove it with the tines of two forks and drop it onto a sheet of wax paper.
- If the coating thickens too much, reheat it a little, perhaps using a microwave. When all the truffles are dipped, you can serve them right away. If they will be stored or transported, refrigerate them awhile longer

first. 30 servings.

Côte de Veau Flambées À La Crème
(Veal Chops in Cream)

Ingredients
- 4 veal loin chops
- 1 ½ TB butter
- 1 TB oil
- 2 TB brandy, warmed
- 2 TB white wine
- 1 tsp potato starch (or cornstarch)
- 1 TB cold water
- 1 cup heavy cream

Preparation
- In a heavy skillet heat together 1 1/2 tablespoons of butter and 1 tablespoon of oil. Wipe the chops dry and brown them in the fat, over a brisk fire, for about 3 minutes on each side; be careful not to burn the fat.
- Season the chops with salt and pepper, cover the skillet, lower the heat, and continue cooking for 15 to 20 minutes, or until tender.
- Then pour 2 tablespoons of warmed brandy over the chops, set it ablaze, and shake the pan back and forth until the flame dies. Remove the chops to a hot serving dish and keep them warm.
- Add 1 or 2 tablespoons of white wine to the pan and stir in all the brown juices. Blend 1 teaspoon of potato starch with 1 tablespoon of cold water and stir in 1 cup of heavy cream.
- Add this to the pan, season the sauce, simmer it, stirring, until it is slightly thickened, and pour it over the chops. Serves 4.

Vegetable Cassoulet

Ingredients

STOCK
- 1 cup dried white haricot beans, soaked overnight
- 3 cups water
- 1 stalk celery cut into three inch pieces
- 2 sprigs fresh thyme
- 2 sprigs fresh rosemary
- 2 sprigs fresh sage
- 1 bay leaf
- 6 black peppercorns

STEW
- 5 TB olive oil
- 1 clove garlic, crushed
- 1 cup pearl onions, peeled
- 2 cups carrots, chopped
- 1 fennel bulb, trimmed and finely chopped
- 3 cups fresh mushrooms, chopped
- 1 medium globe eggplant, coarsely chopped
- 2 ripe tomatoes, peeled, seeded and chopped
- 1 TB fresh thyme, chopped
- 1 TB fresh rosemary, chopped
- ½ cup dry white wine
- ½ cup tomato juice
- ⅓ cup red lentils

TOPPING
- 1 cup freshly grated parmesan cheese
- 1 cup fresh whole wheat bread crumbs

Preparation

- Drain the soaked beans, place in a 3-quart saucepan, and pour in the water. Tie the celery, thyme, rosemary, sage, bay leaf, and peppercorns in a small piece of cheesecloth and add to the pan.
- Bring to a boil and cook over high heat for 10 minutes, then reduce the heat, cover, and simmer gently for 45 to 50 minutes, until the beans are tender. Discard the cheesecloth rag, reserve the beans, and strain the stock into a clean saucepan.
- Bring to a boil and reduce to 1 1/2 cups. Reserve Preheat the oven to 375F. Lightly oil a shallow ovenproof dish with a 2- quart capacity. For the stew, heat 2 tablespoons of the oil in a large skillet and sauté the garlic, onions, carrots, and fennel for 10 minutes, or until lightly browned.

- Remove with a slotted spoon and drain on paper towels. Add the remaining oil to the pan and stir-fry the mushrooms, eggplant, tomatoes, thyme, and rosemary for 5 minutes. Return the onion mixture to the pan, add the wine, and cook over high heat until most of the juice is evaporated.
- Stir in the tomato juice, lentils, and reserved stock and simmer, uncovered, over a low heat for 15 minutes. Add the reserved beans, cover, and simmer gently for 10 minutes more.
- Spoon the stew into the prepared dish, sprinkle the cheese and bread crumbs on top, and bake for 30 minutes, until bubbling and golden. Serve hot. Serves 6 to 8.

Venison Stew

Ingredients
- 4 lb venison, cut in 2" chunks
- 1 carrot, sliced
- 1 small onion, quartered
- ½ stalk celery, sliced
- ¼ tsp dried thyme or ¾ tsp fresh thyme
- salt (or black pepper)
- ⅛ tsp cayenne pepper
- 4 cups California petite syrah or full-bodied red wine
- 1 ½ tsp wine vinegar
- 2 ½ TB corn oil, or more if needed
- 2 TB white flour
- 1 cup water
- Caramelized Pears (optional)

Preparation
- Two to 4 days ahead, in a mixing bowl just large enough to hold meat and vegetables, toss venison, carrot, onion, and celery together. Add thyme, salt, cayenne, wine, and vinegar.
- Cover and marinate in a cool place (50 to 55F) or in warmest part of refrigerator for 2 to 4 days, turning meat and vegetables every day. Drain meat and vegetables in a colander for about 30 minutes, reserving marinade.
- Sort out vegetables from meat and set vegetables aside. Dry meat on towels. In a large, heavy frying pan, heat a thin coat of corn oil over medium heat. Add meat in several batches, being careful not to overcrowd, and sauté until brown, about 5 minutes.

- Transfer meat to a stew pot. In the same frying pan, sauté vegetables for about 5 minutes. Add more corn oil if necessary. Add sautéed vegetables to meat and season with salt and pepper.
- Heat oven to 300F. For the brown roux, add flour to fat in frying pan. Add more corn oil if necessary to make 2 tablespoons. Stir with a wooden spoon and cook until roux is nut brown, 3 to 5 minutes. Strain reserved marinade over roux and quickly whisk it together. Add water and bring to a boil. Strain liquid into the pot with the meat.
- Cover pot tightly and bake on middle shelf of oven for 3 1/2 hours, until meat is very tender. Transfer meat and vegetables with a slotted spoon to a heated serving dish, cover, and keep warm.
- To degrease and thicken sauce, put pot half on burner and let surface that is over the burner come to a boil. Surface of pot off the burner should stand still. Lower heat if it's moving.
- Occasionally, skim and degrease the non-heated surface. Cook in this manner until sauce thickens and becomes shiny, about 30 minutes. Serve stew and pass sauce and pears separately.

Vinaigrette Marinade

Ingredients
- 1 cup olive oil
- ¼ cup red wine vinegar
- 1 TB lemon juice
- ¼ tsp mustard
- 2 cloves garlic, minced
- 4 TB parsley, minced
- ½ tsp oregano, crumbled
- ½ tsp marjoram, crumbled
- 1 tsp thyme, crumbled
- 1 tsp fresh-ground black pepper
- 1 tsp salt

Preparation
- Whip vinegar into oil and add the rest of the ingredients. Mix well and marinate meat in refrigerator for at least 3 hours. Yields: 2 cups

Wild Mushroom Sauce

Ingredients
- 1 TB butter
- 2 medium shallots, chopped
- Pinch of cracked black pepper
- 1 cup wild mushrooms, sliced
- 1 cup domestic mushrooms, your choice, sliced
- 1 tsp fresh sage, chopped
- ¼ cup marsala
- 1 TB butter
- salt, to taste
- pepper, to taste
- 1 ½ TB fresh sage, chopped

Preparation
- Heat pan. Add butter and shallots. Sauté 1 minute then add cracked black pepper and fresh mushrooms. Sauté about 5 to 7 minutes at a high heat.
- Add fresh sage and sauté 30 seconds more. Deglaze pan with marsala wine. Reduce to syrup then add demi-glaze. This demi-glaze will thicken quickly, it has been already reduced.
- When the sauce is ready it will be thick enough to coat the back of a spoon. Before service, bring the sauce to a boil then swirl in the remaining butter, salt and pepper to taste. ENJOY! Yields 1 1/2 cups.

###

Part 5: German Recipes

Germans, *(in addition to sauerkraut!)* *t*end to eat heavy and hearty meals that include ample portions of meat and bread. Potatoes are a staple food, and each region has its own favorite ways of preparing them. Some Germans eat potatoes with pears, bacon, and beans.

Germans from the capital city of Berlin eat potatoes with bacon and spicy sausage. Sauerbraten is a large roast made of pork, beef, or veal that is popular throughout Germany, and is flavored in different ways depending on the region. In the Rhine River area, it is flavored with raisins, but is usually cooked with a variety of savory spices and vinegar. Fruit (instead of vegetables) is often combined with meat dishes to add a sweet and sour taste to the meal. Throughout Germany desserts made with apples are very popular.

A Different Sauerbraten

Ingredients
- 4-6 slices bacon
- 1 beef roast
- flour
- 4 carrots
- 4 celery stalks
- 3 onions
- 8 oz sour cream
- 3 bay leaves
- 1 salt and pepper, to taste

Preparation
- Cook bacon in a large Dutch oven and add cleaned veggies (carrots and celery cut into two to three pieces per stick and onions cut in half and torn apart).
- Brown veggies thoroughly. Roll roast in flour, salt, and pepper mixture. Add roast to pot and brown. (remove veggies) Return veggies to pot and add water to cover.
- Add bay leaves and simmer 3 to 5 hours. Remove roast and bay leaves. Mix remainder (liquid and veggies) in blender with sour cream to desired taste.
- Pour gravy over roast and serve with knodel and rotkohl. Panni brand Knodel (potato dumplings) mix can be found in the specialty food aisle and is easy to prepare.
-

Apfelpfannkuchen
(Apple Pancakes)

Ingredients
- ⅔ cup flour (unbleached)
- 2 tsp sugar
- ¼ tsp salt
- 4 large eggs, beaten
- 1//2 cup milk
- 2 cups apple (slices)
- ¾ cup butter (or margarine)
- 2 TB sugar
- ¼ tsp cinnamon

Preparation

- Sift together the flour, 2 tsp sugar, and the salt.
- Beat eggs and milk together. Gradually add flour mixture; beat until smooth.
- Sauté apples in 1/4 c of butter until tender.
- Mix 2 TB sugar and the cinnamon together; toss with apples.
- Melt 2 TB butter in a 6-inch diameter, deep fry pan.
- Pour in the batter to a depth of about 1/4-inch.
- When set, place 1/4 of the apples on top; cover with more batter.
- Fry pancake until lightly browned on both sides. Keep warm.
- Repeat the procedure 3 times, until all batter and apples are used.
- Serve immediately. Serves 4.

Apfelkraut
(German Homemade Apple Syrup)

Ingredients

- 10 kg sweet, ripe apples
- 1 vanilla stick
- 15g pectin

Preparation

- Wash, quarter, core the apples, cut into coarse slices. Boil the apples in nearly no water until they are cooked.
- Put the apples on a suitable cloth and squeeze the juice out. Boil the juice with the sliced vanilla stick and the pectin.

Apfelstrudel
(Apple Strudel)

Ingredients

- 6 cups tart apples, sliced
- ¾ cup raisins
- 1 TB grated lemon rind
- ¾ cup sugar
- 2 tsp cinnamon
- ¾ cup ground almonds
- 8 oz fillo leaves, thawed (1/2 box)
- 1 ¾ cups butter, melted (not margarine)
- 1 cup bread crumbs, finely crushed

Preparation
- Mix apples with raisins, lemon rind, sugar, cinnamon, and almonds. Set aside. Place 1 fillo leaf on a kitchen towel and brush with melted butter.
- Place a second leaf on top and brush with butter again. Repeat until 5 leaves have been used, using about 1/2 c of butter. Cook and stir bread crumbs with 1/4 c of butter until lightly browned.
- Sprinkle 3/4 cup crumbs on the layered fillo leaves. Mound 1/2 of the filling in a 3-inch strip along the narrow end of the fillo, leaving a 2-inch border.
- Lift towel, using it to roll leaves over apples, jelly roll fashion. Brush top of the strudel with butter and sprinkle with 2 T crumbs.
- Repeat the entire procedure for the second strudel. Bake the strudels at 400 degrees F. for 20 to 25 minutes, until browned. Makes 2 strudels, 6 to 8 servings each.

Apple and Cream Kuchen

Ingredients
- ½ tsp salt
- 2 cups unbleached flour
- **MILK FILLING**
- 1 TB lemon juice
- ¾ cup sugar
- 8 oz cream cheese, softened
- 1 pack active dry yeast
- 4 TB sugar
- ¼ cup butter (or margarine)
- 1 large egg
- 3 cups tart apples, sliced
- 1 tsp cinnamon
- 2 TB unbleached flour
- 1 large egg

Preparation
- CAKE: Mix yeast, salt, 4 T sugar, and 3/4 cup flour. Add butter to milk. Heat until very warm (120-130 degrees F.). Gradually add milk to flour mixture.
- Beat for 2 minutes. Add egg and 1/2 cup flour. Beat with an electric mixer on high speed for 2 minutes. Mix in enough flour to form soft dough.
- Knead for 5 to 10 minutes, until dough is shiny and elastic. Place in greased bowl and let rise for 1 hour or until doubled in bulk.

- Pat dough into well-greased 10-inch spring form pan pressing the dough 1 1/2 inches up the sides of the pan.
- FILLING: Toss apples with lemon juice, cinnamon, 1/4 cup sugar, and 2 T of flour. Arrange in rows on top of the dough.
- Beat together cream cheese, 1/2 cup sugar, and egg. Spread over apples. Let rise in warm place for 1 hour. Bake at 350 degrees F. for 30 minutes. Best when served warm.

Bavarian Potato Salad

Ingredients
- 4 cups potatoes, peeled and sliced ¼ inch thick
- ½ tsp salt
- ⅓ cup onion, chopped
- 2 TB lemon juice
- 2 cups chicken broth
- ¼ cup vegetable oil
- ½ tsp sugar
- pepper to taste

Preparation
- Boil potatoes in broth with 1/4 t salt for 5 to 8 minutes, until tender. Drain.
- Toss warm potatoes with vegetable oil and onions.
- Dissolve remaining 1/4 t salt and the sugar in lemon juice. Pour over potatoes.
- Marinate salad 1 to 2 hours before serving. Serve at room temperature. Serves 4.

Braised Red Cabbage

Ingredients
- 1 red cabbage, julienned
- 2 TB vegetable oil (or corn oil)
- 2 TB cider vinegar, red wine vinegar or rice vinegar
- ½ cup onions, chopped
- 1 apple, peeled, cored and cut into thin slices
- 2 TB honey (or brown sugar)
- 1/2 cup Chicken stock (or vegetable broth)
- 2 whole cloves
- 2 TB butter

- pepper
- salt

Preparation
- Examine and clean the cabbage. Discard any tough or wilted leaves, cut away and discard the core. Cut the remaining leaves into thin julienne.
- Heat the oil in a heavy skillet and add the onion and cabbage and sauté, stirring, until wilted.
- Add the apple slices, broth, vinegar, honey, cloves, salt and pepper. Blend well. Cover and cook 15 minutes, stirring often.
- Uncover and simmer until liquid reduces by half. Add butter, stir and blend well.

Bratwurst in Beer, Berlin Style

Ingredients
- 12 bratwurst (or pork sausage)
- 2 TB butter (or margarine)
- 1 ¼ cups beer
- salt and pepper to taste
- 1 TB flour
- 2 medium onions, peeled and sliced
- 2 bay leaves
- 3 TB parsley, chopped

Preparation
- Place Bratwurst in a saucepan and cover with boiling water. Cook 3 minutes; drain. Melt butter in a skillet; add bratwurst to brown.
- Remove to a warm plate. Pour off all except 2 TB fat. Add onions; sauté until tender. Return sausages to skillet. Add bay leaves, beer, salt and pepper. Cook slowly for 15 minutes
- Add more beer during cooking, if needed. Remove Bratwurst to a warm platter. Mix flour with a little cold water; stir into hot liquid.
- Cook, stirring, until liquid is a thick sauce; remove bay leaves. Add parsley; pour over sausage. Serve with mashed potatoes and red cabbage.
- Slowly simmer for about 20 minutes. Meanwhile cook the green beans in salted water until al dente.
- Drain water. Stir green beans into gravy and let steep for a few minutes before serving.   Serves 4.

Crisp German Meatballs

Ingredients
- ½ lb ground pork sausage
- ¼ cup onion, chopped
- 1 16 oz can chopped sauerkraut, drained
- 2 TB bread crumbs, dry and fine
- 1 pkg cream cheese, softened
- 2 TB parsley
- 1 tsp prepared mustard
- ¼ tsp garlic salt
- ⅛ tsp pepper
- 1 cup mayonnaise
- ¼ cup prepared mustard
- 2 eggs
- ¼ cup milk
- ½ cup flour
- 1 cup bread crumbs, fine
- vegetable oil

Preparation
- Combine sausage and onion in a large pan; cook till sausage is browned, stirring for it to crumble. Drain well. Stir in kraut and 2 T breadcrumbs.
- Combine cream cheese and next 4 ingredients in large bowl; add sausage mixture, stirring well. Cover and let stand for 2 hrs.
- Combine mayonnaise and mustard; set aside.
- Combine eggs and milk in a bowl; set aside.
- Shape sausage mixture into 3/4" balls; roll in flour. Dip each ball in reserved egg mixture; roll balls in breadcrumbs.
- Pour oil to a depth of 2" into Dutch oven; heat to 375F. Fry a few at a time, 2 minutes or till golden brown.
- Drain on paper towel. Serve with mayonnaise mixture. Yields 5 dozen

False Hare
(German Meatloaf)

Ingredients
- ½ lb lean ground beef
- 1 medium onion, chopped
- 3 TB cold water

- ½ tsp salt
- 1 tsp prepared mustard
- 3 hard cooked eggs, peeled

VEGETABLE OIL SAUCE
- 1 tsp cornstarch
- ½ cup sour cream
- ½ lb lean ground pork
- 3 TB bread crumbs
- 2 large eggs
- 1 tsp paprika
- 2 TB chopped parsley
- 4 strips bacon
- 1 cup beef broth
- ¼ cup hot water
- ¼ cup water

Preparation

- Thoroughly mix ground meats, onion, bread crumbs, 3 T cold water, and eggs. Flavor with salt, paprika, mustard, and parsley. Blend ingredients thoroughly.
- Flatten out meat mixture in the shape of a square, (8 X 8-inches). Arrange whole hard-boiled eggs in a row along the middle of the meat.
- Fold sides of meat patty over the eggs. Shape meat carefully into a loaf resembling a flat bread loaf. Occasionally rinse hands in cold water to prevent sticking.
- Cube 2 strips bacon; cook in a Dutch oven about 2 minutes. Carefully add the vegetable oil; heat. Place meatloaf in the Dutch oven and cook until browned on all sides.
- Cut remaining bacon strips in half and arrange over the top of the meatloaf. Place uncovered Dutch oven in a preheated oven for about 45 minutes.
- While meat is baking, gradually pour hot beef broth over the top of the meatloaf; brush occasionally with pan drippings.
- When done remove meat to a preheated platter and keep it warm. Add 1/4 cup of hot water to pan and scrape particles from the bottom.
- Bring to a gentle boil and add cornstarch that has been mixed with 1/4 cup water. Cook until bubbly and thick. Remove from heat and stir in sour cream.
- Reheat to warm. Season with salt and pepper if desired. Serve the sauce separately.

Haselnusstorte
(Hazelnut Torte)

Ingredients
- ¾ cup sugar
- 5 large eggs, separated
- 6 TB water
- 1 ¾ cups cake flour, sifted
- 1 tsp baking powder
- 1 ½ cups hazelnuts (filberts), ground
- 1 tsp vanilla extract
- 2 TB confectioners' sugar
- 1 cup heavy cream, whipped
- fresh strawberries if desired

Preparation
- Beat the egg yolks and sugar until very light, about 5 minutes. Slowly add the water. Sift the flour and baking powder together. Mix with 1 cup of nuts.
- Fold the flour mixture into the egg yolks. Beat the egg whites until soft peaks form. Gently fold the whites into the batter.
- Pour into a greased and floured 10-inch springform pan. Bake at 375F for 30 minutes or until cake is done. Cool cake on wire rack.
- When completely cooled, split the cake into 2 layers.
- Fold the vanilla, confectioners' sugar, and remaining 1/2 cup of nuts into the whipped cream. Spread whipped cream between the 2 cake layers and on top of the cake. Chill until serving time. Garnish with strawberries if desired.

Hasenoehrle
(Rabbit Ears)

Ingredients
- 3 1/2 cups flour
- 1 dash salt
- 1 egg
- As much baking powder as will fit on the tip of a knife
- 1 spoon clarified butter
- ⅔ cup plus ¼ warm milk
- sugar to taste
- ground cinnamon to taste

- fat for frying

Preparation
- Combine the flour, salt, egg, milk, and clarified butter and knead into firm noodle dough. Let rest for one hour. On a floured pastry board, roll out to the thickness of the back of a knife.
- With a knife or pastry wheel, cut into rectangles and deep fry until golden brown. While still hot, dust with sugar and cinnamon, and serve. Serves 4.

Hot German Potato Salad

Ingredients
- 10 medium potatoes, cooked and sliced
- 1 onion, chopped
- ¼ cup water
- 2 TB whole-wheat flour
- 1 TB honey
- 1 tsp tamari soy sauce
- ½ tsp celery seed
- 1 dash ground pepper (optional)
- ¾ cup water
- ½ cup vinegar

Preparation
- Sauté the onion in 1/4 cup water over medium heat until tender and beginning to brown. Stir in flour, honey, tamari, and celery seed.
- Mix well until smooth. Stir in water and vinegar. Heat to boiling, stirring constantly. Add potatoes, stirring carefully. Heat through. Serve hot.

Pot Roast
With Sour Cream Sauce

Ingredients
- 1 tsp salt
- 1 medium onion, peeled and sliced
- 1 cup dry red wine
- ½ tsp salt
- 2 TB all-purpose flour
- 4 lb top (or bottom) round of beef

- ¼ tsp black pepper
- ½ cup sour cream

Preparation

- To Cook: Sprinkle 1 teas. Salt in a large skillet, set over med. high heat and brown the roast well on all sides. Remove roast to slow cooker.
- Add the onion to the skillet and brown lightly, stirring often. Pour in the wine: scrape up pan juices and turn into the slow cooker with the salt and pepper.
- Cover, turn to Low and cook 10-12 hours. Before Serving: Skim 2 Tab. Fat from the liquid in the cooker and heat in a medium skillet over low heat.
- Stir in the flour to make a smooth paste. Then add the cooking liquid all at once; stir continuously until the sauce is smooth and has thickened - about 5-7 min.
- Remove skillet from heat; stir in the sour cream. Serve sauce over the pot roast.

Sauerbraten
(Sweet Sour Beef)

Ingredients

- 3 ½ lb bottom round
- 2 cups wine vinegar (heated)
- 2 cups water
- 1 ½ tsp salt
- 2 TB parsley
- 1 tsp pepper
- 2 TB sugar
- 1 onion, sliced
- 1 bay leaf
- 3 TB butter
- 2 TB flour
- 2 TB cold water
- 1 cup beef stock
- 6 gingersnaps

Preparation

- Heat 2 cups water and vinegar together until hot. Place meat in crock covered with vinegar and water. [Do NOT use a metal pot!] Add salt, parsley, pepper, sugar, and onion.
- Cover and refrigerate for 3 days, turning daily. Drain marinade and

reserve. Lightly flour meat. Brown well in butter in kettle.
- Add onion slices and 3 cups marinade. Cover and simmer until tender. Remove meat to a hot serving dish and keep warm. Skim fat off liquid. Mix flour and water and stir into pan. Add stock.

Sauerbraten Klopse
(Sauerbraten Meatballs)

Ingredients
- 1 lb lean ground beef
- ¼ cup milk
- ¼ cup dry bread crumbs
- ⅛ tsp ground cloves
- ⅛ tsp ground allspice
- ½ tsp salt
- pepper, to taste
- 2 TB vegetable oil
- ½ cup vinegar
- ¾ tsp ground ginger
- 1 bay leaf
- 4 TB brown sugar
- 2 TB unbleached flour

Preparation
- Mix beef, milk, crumbs, cloves, allspice, salt and pepper. Form into meatballs. Brown meatballs in hot oil. Drain off fat. Add 1 cup water, vinegar, ginger, bay leaf, and brown sugar
- Cover and simmer 1/2 hour. Skim off fat. Remove meatballs and keep them warm. Mix flour and 2 T water. Slowly stir into the pan juices to make gravy. Pour gravy over meatballs. Serve with buttered noodles.

Sauerkraut Soup

Ingredients
- 1 large jar sauerkraut
- 2 apples
- 1 onion
- 1 tsp caraway seed
- ½ head fresh white cabbage

- 1 smoked pig's knuckle or 1 chunk of ham
- salt and pepper
- 1 cup apple juice
- 1 cup water
- 1 garnish
- 2 small boiled potatoes

Preparation

- Simplest recipe for sauerkraut soup: Rinse the s-k, 1 large jar or can, in running cold water. Put in a stainless steel or iron (not aluminum) pot. Chop into chunks 2 apples. Add. Chop 1 onion.
- Add. Add 1 teaspoon of caraway seed. Chop 1/2 head of fresh white cabbage. Add. Add 1 smoked pig's knuckle. Salt and pepper to taste. Add 1 cup apple juice (optional) and 1 cup or more water.
- Simmer covered at least for 45 minutes (time varies, depending on brand of kraut; some is so processed that it may need less time than that!) Instead of knuckle, uncooked ham chunk may be added.
- Good, smoked ham would be wasted but not unpalatable. Delicious soup is good if served with boiled, buttered and seasoned potatoes on the side.
- If you wish to prepare more soup, for more people than the 2 of you, a whole shoulder can be used with 3 cans or jars of sauerkraut, giving enough meat for everyone.
- (For a large shoulder to cook thoroughly you would need over an hour of cooking time, if the shoulder had not been precooked. Otherwise, the 30-45 minutes is enough. But you taste and decide!)

Schnecken

Ingredients

- 1 Cottage cheese and oil pastry
- 1 oz soft butter (or margarine) for brushing
- 2 ½ oz raisins, washed and drained well
- 1 ¾ oz almonds, blanched

FILLING

- 2 TB sugar, heaping
- 1 pkg vanillin sugar
- 1 ¾ oz currants, washed and drained well, chopped finely

ICING

- 6 oz icing (powdered) sugar
- 2 TB hot water (approx)

Preparation

- Roll out the pastry to a rectangle 14x18in. (45x35cm) and brush with the fat. For the Filling: mix together the filling ingredients and distribute evenly over the pastry. Starting from the shorter side, roll up like a Swiss roll.
- Then use a sharp knife to cut off slices about 1 1/4 in thick. Lay these on a greased baking sheet and flatten slightly. OVEN: preheat oven for 5 min at 400F. BAKING TIME: 15-20 minutes.
- For the icing: sieve the icing sugar (powdered sugar) and blend with as much of the water as will five a good coating consistency. Ice the schnecken while still hot.

Schweineschnitzel

Ingredients
- 6 Servings
- 4 (6-ounce) Pork cutlets
- Freshly ground -pepper to taste and salt
- Flour for dredging
- 1 Egg
- 1 tsp Water
- 1 cup Fresh bread crumbs
- 4 Tsp Butter (or margarine)
- 1 Tsp Capers
- Lemon wedges

Preparation
- Pound the cutlets until thin. Sprinkle lightly on both sides with salt and pepper. Dredge them lightly but thoroughly in flour.
- Beat the egg lightly with the water and dip the floured cutlets in the mixture; coat with crumbs. Using the side of a kitchen knife, tap the cutlets lightly so the crumbs will adhere well to the meat.
- Transfer them to a wire rack. Refrigerate for one or two hours. This will help the breading adhere to the cutlets when they are being cooked.
- Heat the butter in a large skillet and, when it is hot but not brown or smoking, sauté the cutlets in it until they are golden brown on both sides.
- Arrange the cutlets on a heated serving platter and garnish with the capers and lemon wedges. Serve immediately. Serves four.

Der Wiener Schnitzel

Ingredients
- 4 oz veal (per person)
- Olive oil
- Shortening
- Salt
- Flour
- 1 Egg
- 1 Fine dry bread crumbs
- 6 servings

Preparation
- Trim all fat from veal. Pound each slice as thin as possible (about 1/8 inch thick). Make small vertical cuts all around the edges of the veal. Salt each slice.
- Dip first into a soup plate containing flour, and shake off excess; next into a soup plate of beaten egg; finally into a soup plate containing dried bread crumbs, pressing crumbs well in with the palm of your hand, then shaking off excess.
- Fry in deep fat, half olive oil, half melted shortening, so hot that it smokes, for 2 to 3 minutes on each side, or until heat is right when the breading ripples golden brown.
- Schnitzel is done and tender when a fork goes right through the meat. Serve garnished with lemon wedges and potatoes or salad as a side dish.

Wild Pig on Sauerkraut

Ingredients
- 2 ½ b. wild or tame pork shoulder rolled and tied up.
- 1 3/4 oz Butter
- Salt & pepper to taste
- 4 Smashed juniper berries
- ¼ lb sauerkraut
- 2 Bay leaves
- 6 Whole juniper berries
- 2 Apples
- 1 cup White wine
- 6 slices Canadian bacon
- 1 3/4 oz Crisco

Preparation

- Melt butter and fry pork on all sides in it. Add the salt, pepper and smashed juniper berries. Heat oven to 225 C and bake the pork for 1/2 hour long, basting it with its juices a couple of times.
- Heat the Crisco in a pot and sauté the sauerkraut shortly in it. Add bay leaves, juniper berries, the grated apples and the wine. Let simmer, on medium heat, for 30 minutes.
- Put the pork on top of the sauerkraut and pour the juices all over it. Let it bake for another 35 minutes, at 170 C. Slice pork and serve on top of kraut with beer.

Zwiebelkuchen
(Onion Pie)

Ingredients

- 1 pkg Active dry yeast
- 1 tsp Sugar
- 1 1/2 tsp Salt
- 3 cups Unbleached flour
- 1 Tsp Shortening
- 1 cup 120 to 130 Degrees water.
- 6 Cut up slices bacon
- 2 Sliced medium onions
- 1/4 tsp Cumin
- 1/2 tsp salt
- Pepper as desired
- 1 Egg yolk
- 1 cup Sour cream

Preparation

- Mix yeast, sugar, 1 t salt, and 1/2 cup flour. Blend in shortening and warm water. Beat for 2 minutes. Add enough flour to make a soft dough.
- Knead dough until smooth and elastic for about 5 minutes. Place dough in a lightly greased bowl. Cover and let dough rise in a warm place 1/2 hour.
- Pat dough into a lightly greased 12-inch pizza pan or onto a lightly greased baking sheet. Press up edges to make a slight rim.
- Fry bacon until crisp. Remove from grease and drain on absorbent paper.
- Add onions to bacon grease; cook slowly until tender but not brown.
- Sprinkle onion, bacon, cumin, 1/2 t salt and pepper over dough. Bake at 400 Degrees F. for 20 minutes.

- Blend egg yolk and sour cream. Pour over onions. Bake for 10 to 15 minutes longer, until golden brown and sour cream is set. Serve warm.

###

Part 6: Greek Recipes

Greek cuisine - "Greek" is the traditional cuisine of Greece, a Mediterranean sharing characteristics with the cuisines of Italy, the Balkans, Turkey and the Levant. . Contemporary Greek cookery makes wide use of olive oil, vegetables and herbs, grains and bread, wine, fish, and various meats, including poultry, rabbit and pork. Also important are olives, cheese, zucchini, and yogurt. . The desserts are dominated by nuts and honey. Many dishes use a phyllo pastry.

Adreana's Greek Pasta Salad

Ingredients
- 1 lb Rotini
- 1 lb Breasts boneless skinless chicken
- 3 Stalks chopped celery
- 1 Chopped red bell pepper
- 2 1/4 oz Sliced black olives
- 4 oz Drained & Crumbled Feta cheese
- 3 Green onions finely sliced
- 16 oz Italian salad dressing

Preparation
- Cook chicken in water to cover with 1 bay leaf. Bring to boil and cook for 30 min or until juices run clear.
- Cool and remove skins or, you can cook chicken in frying pan until cooked through. Cut into bite size pieces.
- Cook noodles and drains. Add all ingredients and mix well. I use only about half the bottle of dressing and then put the rest on the table if someone wants more. Serve warm or cold.

Bastilla

Ingredients
- 1 lb chicken breasts (or thighs)
- 1 medium chopped onion
- 3 cups preferably-homemade chicken stock
- 1/2 cup Chopped fresh parsley
- 1 Stick cinnamon (3 inches -long)
- 1/2 tsp Ground ginger
- 1/8 tsp Pepper
- 1/4 tsp Saffron threads
- 3 Eggs
- 8 Sheets phyllo thawed dough
- 1 Tsp Melted butter
- 1 Tsp Granulated white sugar
- 1 tsp Cinnamon
- 2/3 cup Chopped blanched almonds
- Powdered sugar for garnish
- Cinnamon for garnish

Preparation
- Preheat oven to 425 F. In a large kettle add the chicken, stock, parsley, cinnamon stick, ginger, pepper and saffron.
- Bring to a boil over high heat. Cover, reduce heat and simmer until chicken is tender, about 30 to 45 minutes.
- Lift chicken from stock and let stand until cool enough to handle. Remove and discard bones and skin. Shred the meat into bite size pieces.
- Bring the broth to a boil over medium heat. Lightly beat eggs and pour slowly into the stock stirring until curds form, about 1 to 2 minutes.
- Pour mixture through a fine strainer placed over a bowl. Let stand until well drained. Reserve stock for soup or other uses. Discard the cinnamon stick.
- Stack phyllo; keep covered to prevent drying out. Brush some of the butter on the bottom and sides of a 10-inch deep pie pan.
- Overlap 6 sheets in the pan to cover bottom and extend 8 to 10 inches beyond edge.
- Brush phyllo with butter. Sprinkle sugar and second measure of cinnamon over phyllo. Top evenly with the chicken.
- Spread egg mixture over chicken, and then sprinkle with almonds. Fold the edges of the phyllo over the filling and brush top with butter.
- Fold remaining 2 sheets of phyllo in half crosswise and place on pie. Tuck edges inside pan and brush top with butter.
- Bake uncovered in a 425 oven for 20 minutes, or until golden brown. Shake pan to loosen pie. Hold an unrimmed baking sheet loosely over the top of the pie and invert pan.
- Lift off pan, return pie to the oven and bake until golden brown; about 10 minutes. Invert pie onto platter. Let stand 5 minutes.
- Sift powdered sugar generously over top and then decorate with crisscrossing lines of ground cinnamon.

Bear Steaks w/Greek Seasonings

Ingredients
- 2 lb bear steaks
- 1/2 cup Olive oil
- 1/2 cup Lemon juice
- 1 Tsp Garlic powder
- 1 tsp Salt
- 1 tsp Pepper
- 1 tsp Combination of oregano marjoram and rosemary

Preparation
- Trim all visible fat from the bear as it turns rancid rapidly. Whisk the other

ingredients together until emulsified.
- Use the emulsion to marinate the meat for 2-3 hours, refrigerated. Longer marina ding before cooking does not improve the meat as the remaining bear fat will go rancid despite refrigeration.
- Grill, broil or sauté the steaks until well done. Bear should always be thoroughly cooked as a trichinosis precaution.
- Serve immediately. Do not try making gravy from the marinade as it will usually have picked up a gamy taste from the bear meat.

Braised Lamb Shanks in Lemon-Dill Sauce

Ingredients
- 2 Medium chopped onions (2 cups)
- 2 Medium chopped carrots (1 cup)
- 2 Cloves garlic
- 1 Medium leek
- 4 lg About 1 pound lamb shanks sawed crosswise into thirds
- 5 Tsp Olive oil
- 3 Bay leaves
- 3 1/2 cups Fresh chicken stock or canned chicken broth
- 1 tsp Salt
- 3 T Loosely packed fresh dill leaves
- 1/3 cup 2 Lemons
- 2 Eggs
- 1/2 tsp Fresh Ground pepper

Preparation
- Peel onions, carrots, and garlic. Chop and put onions and carrots in a bowl with garlic. Rinse, trim, and chop leek, (using white portion and about 2 inches of the green), and add to the bowl. Pat shanks dry.
- COOKING: Adjust oven rack to middle position and heat oven to 350F. Heat 2 tablespoons of oil in a 5-quart Dutch oven until hot but not smoking
- Working in batches, sear lamb shanks over high heat until they are browned on all sides, about 7 minutes; set shanks aside.
- Discard cooking fat and add remaining oil, vegetables and bay leaves. Cover and sauté over low heat, stirring occasionally, until vegetables are lightly colored, about 15 minutes.
- Return shanks and accumulated juices to the pot along with stock and 1 teaspoon salt. Bring stock to a boil; reduce heat to low, and simmer,

- covered, for 45 minutes.
- Uncover and simmer until lamb is tender, 55-60 minutes. Remove shanks. Strain stock and return it to the pot.
- Bring to a boil, skimming it well, and reduce to 1 3/4 cups. (Can cover and refrigerate shanks in the stock for up to 2 days.)
- SERVING: If made ahead, heat shanks in foil in oven until hot. Bring stock to a boil. Mince dill. Squeeze 1/3 cup lemon juice into a medium bowl, whisk in eggs, and then slowly whisk in hot stock. Stir in dill and 1/2 teaspoon pepper
- Return the shanks to the pot add the lemon-egg mixture and cook over low heat, gently stirring and shaking the pot, until shanks are warmed through and sauce has thickened slightly, about 5 minutes. Do not let sauce simmer or eggs may curdle.

Bulghur Pilaf

Ingredients
- 2 Tsp Butter (or oil)
- 1 sm Chopped onion
- 1/8 tsp Salt
- 1/8 tsp Turmeric
- 1/2 tsp Thyme
- 1 cup Bulgur
- 1 3/4 cup Water
- 1/4 cup Soy sauce (or tamari soy)
- Sauce or 2 cups vegetable beef or chicken stock
- 3/4 cup Frozen sweet peas
- 2 Tsp Grated carrots
- 2 Tsp Chopped celery
- 1 Tsp Chopped raisins (optional)
- 2 Tsp Chopped parsley (optional)
- 4 servings

Preparation
- Sauté onion in butter or oil or combination and add thyme and turmeric. Stir in bulghur and sauté while stirring for 3 minutes. Add liquid and salt and pepper.
- Cover and simmer for 25 minutes and stir in frozen peas, celery and grated carrot. Cover tightly and let sit off of the heat for 5 minutes. (Optional: Stir in chopped parsley and raisins). Serve.

Bechmel Coated Fried Chicken

Ingredients

- 3 cups Chicken stock
- 4 Canned chicken bro Chicken breast halves skinned (1 1/2 pounds)
- Béchamel coating
- 5 Tsp Butter
- 6 Tsp White flour
- 3/4 cup Milk
- 1/4 tsp Thyme salt found white pepper
- 1 Beaten Eggs
- 2 tablespoons water
- 1 cup Dry bread crumbs
- 3 Quarts olive oil for frying

Preparation

- Bring chicken stock to boil in a large saucepan. Add chicken breasts; return stock to boil, cover, and simmer until chicken is cooked through, about 12 minutes.
- Remove chicken breast; reserve 3/4 cup of the chicken stock for the Béchamel Coating. Cool chicken breasts to room temperature. Meanwhile, for the coating, heat butter in a small saucepan.
- Add flour; cook over low heat, stirring constantly until flour is incorporated into the butter, about 30 seconds.
- Continuing to stir constantly, gradually add milk and reserved 3/4 cup chicken stock. Simmer, still stirring constantly, until béchamel thickens, about 2 minutes.
- Stir in thyme and season with 1/4 teaspoon salt and 1/8 teaspoon white pepper or to taste; cool to room temperature.
- Dip each chicken breast in this béchamel, then refrigerate until béchamel is firm, about 1 hour. (Can be refrigerated overnight.)
- TO COOK: Heat oil in a Dutch oven or electric deep fryer to 365F. Dip both sides of each chicken breast into the egg-water mixture, and then dredge in breadcrumbs.
- Dry chicken breasts, turning once, until golden brown, about 5 minutes. Drain chicken breasts on paper towels and serve.

Cabbage Salad

Ingredients

- 1 1/2 lb Green (or Savoy cabbage)
- 1 medium Shredded finely
- 1 medium Grated onion
- 2 T Chopped fresh parsley
- 1/3 cup Olive oil to taste
- 3 Tsp Wine vinegar to taste
- 1 tsp Sugar salt freshly ground pepper to taste
- 1 Green bell pepper for garnish
- Seeded, dribbled, and cut in thin

Preparation

- In a large salad bowl, combine cabbage, onion, and parsley. In a small bowl whisk together oil, vinegar, sugar, salt, and ground pepper.
- Pour dressing over cabbage and toss until thoroughly coated. Arrange bell pepper rings on top. Cover and chill before serving.

Chilies & Garlic in Oil

Ingredients

- 2 lg Red bell peppers
- Seeded and into 1/4" sliced rings
- 3 Fresh pimientos, with stems
- 6 Fresh hot chilies mixture of red green and yellow stems
- 3 Long Italian chilies with stems
- 6 Small boiling onions
- 20 lg Garlic cloves
- 1 lg Onion
- Se note cut into 1/2" rings fresh dill
- 2 cups olive oil
- 6 servings

Preparation

- Place all vegetables in a skillet (with a tight-fitting lid) large enough to hold them in a single layer. Lay dill on top and pour in enough olive oil to cover vegetables in pan. Put pan over moderate heat.
- When oil begins to simmer, reduce heat to lowest possible setting, turn vegetables over once, cover, and cook until boiling onions are quite soft

(45 minutes to 1 hour).
- If you have an electric stove, the lowest setting may not be low enough and you may need to use a heat diffuser. When vegetables are done, remove from heat, leave covered, and serve when cool.

Couscous

Ingredients
- 1 2/3 cup couscous
- 2 cups water
- 2 Tsp Butter
- 1 1/2 tsp Salt

Preparation
- Add butter to boiling water, stir in couscous, cover and cook for three minutes. Turn off heat and let sit for 5 minutes, if fast cooking couscous.
- For regular, let sit for 10-15 minutes. Stir in salt and fluff before serving.

Cucumbers Stuffed w/Feta

Ingredients
- 1/2 cup Crumbled feta cheese
- 1 Tsp Mayonnaise
- 2 squirts Worcestershire sauce
- 4 Small chilled cucumbers
- 1 Tsp Garnish minced fresh parsley

Preparation
- In a small bowl combine cheese, mayonnaise, and Worcestershire sauce; Mix well.
- Quarter cucumbers vertically
- Stuff with feta mixture

Fried Beer Batter Coated Strawberries

Ingredients
- 4 Servings apricot sauce
- 1/4 cup Apricot jam

- 1/2 Tsp Dark rum
- 2 Quarts Pure olive oil for frying
- 2/3 cup White flour
- 2/3 cup Beer
- 1 1/2 Tsp Granulated sugar
- 16 Large strawberries
- 2 Tsp Sugar powdered

Preparation

- For the sauce, bring apricot jam, rum, and 1/4 cup water to boil in a small saucepan. Simmer to blend flavors, about 4 minutes; cover and keep sauce warm.
- TO COOK: For the strawberries, heat oil in a Dutch oven or electric deep fryer to 365F. Mix flour, beer, and sugar in a small bowl. Dip each strawberry in this batter just before placing it in the hot oil.
- Working in batches to avoid overcrowding, fry strawberries until golden brown, 2 to 3 minutes. Drain strawberries on paper towels.
- TO SERVE: Dust strawberries with confectioners' sugar and serve immediately with Apricot Sauce.

Fried Cinnamon Pastries w/Honey Glaze

Ingredients

- 1/2 cup Vegetable oil
- 4 Strips lemon zest 2 by-1/2-inch
- 2 1/2-inch Sticks cinnamon
- 1/2 cup Dry white wine
- 2 cup White flour
- 1 cup Honey
- 3 Tsp Sugar powdered
- 1/4 tsp Ground cinnamon
- 2 Quarts olive oil for-frying

Preparation

- Cook vegetable oil and strips of lemon zest in a small saucepan over medium-high heat until lemon zest is dark brown, about 10 minutes.
- Remove and discard zest. Cool vegetable oil slightly, then add cinnamon sticks.
- Cover the pan with plastic wrap and let oil stand overnight. Then remove and discard cinnamon sticks.
- Mix cinnamon-flavored oil, the white wine, and the flour in a medium bowl; knead this dough in the bowl until is smooth, about 2 minutes. the

- dough into a disk, wrap it in plastic wrap, and let it rest 30 minutes.
- On a floured work surface, roll the dough into a 14- by 10-inch rectangle, about 1/8-inch thick.
- Cut dough rectangle into seventy 2- by 1-inch strips; cover the dough strips with a kitchen towel and let them rest again for 30 minutes.
- TO COOK: Bring the honey and 1/4 cup water to boil in a small saucepan; simmer 15 minutes. Cover this honey mixture and keep it warm.
- Mix confectioners' sugar and cinnamon in a small bowl; set this cinnamon- sugar aside.
- Heat the oil in a Dutch oven or electric deep fryer to 365F. Working in batches to avoid overcrowding, fry the dough strips until they are golden brown, 2 to 3 minutes.
- Place fried pastries on paper towels. Dip each pastry in the honey mixture, then transfer pastry to a wire rack to allow excess honey to drain.
- Cool to room temperature, then dust pastries with the cinnamon-sugar. (Can be stored in an airtight container up to 3 days.)

Fried Swordfish With Mediterranean Spices

Ingredients
- 1/2 cup White wine vinegar
- 1/2 tsp Paprika
- 1/2 tsp Dried red pepper flakes
- 1/2 tsp Oregano
- 1/2 tsp Ground cumin
- 1/2 tsp Thyme
- 3 Medium minced cloves garlic
- 1 Bay leaf salt
- 1 1/2 lb swordfish cut in 1" pieces
- 3 Quarts olive oil for frying
- 1/2 cup White flour
- 4 Servings

Preparation
- Mix first 8 ingredients plus 1/2 teaspoon salt in a medium non reactive bowl. Add swordfish pieces; toss to coat. Cover and let stand at room temperature at least 1 hour. (Can be marinated up to 3 hours.)
- TO COOK: Heat oven to 200F. Heat oil in a Dutch oven or electric deep fryer to 365F. Transfer swordfish from marinade to a sieve. Drain swordfish; discard marinade.

- Pat swordfish pieces dry with paper towels, then dredge in flour. Working in batches to avoid overcrowding, fry swordfish until golden brown, 2 to 3 minutes.
- Drain swordfish pieces on paper towel; transfer to a heatproof platter and keep them warm in the oven until ready to serve. (Can be kept warm in the oven up to 1/2 hour.)

Ganza

Ingredients
- 3 Eggs
- 3/4 cup Milk
- 1/8 tsp Salt
- 1/2 tsp Granulated white sugar
- 1 1/2 cup White wheat flour
- 2 Tsp Brown sugar sprinkle over mixture before serving

Preparation
- Mix all ingredients in a blender and pour into 1/4 inch of oil on medium heat setting in a cast iron pan.
- Using two forks crises-cross through the mixture until golden brown.

Greek Easter Lamb or Kid

Ingredients
- 8 Servings
- 5 lb Kid leg of lamb
- 1 tsp Salt
- 2 Tsp Fresh oregano leaves
- 2 tsp Dried oregano leaves
- 2 Tsp Fresh basil leaves
- 2 tsp Dried basil leaves
- 2 Tsp Fresh mint leaves
- 2 tsp Dried mint leaves
- 3 Tsp Fresh rosemary leaves
- 1 1/2 Tsp Dried rosemary
- 1 Tsp Fresh thyme leaves
- 1 tsp Dried thyme leaves
- 4 lg Peeled Coarsely mince garlic cloves Crushed
- 1 cup Olive oil

- 6 Tsp Fresh lemon juice

Preparation
- Two to four hours before roasting, remove meat from refrigerator. Trim all outside fat and prominent sinews.
- In a food processor, blender, or electric mince puree together salt, oregano, basil, mint, rosemary, thyme, and garlic. (Add 1 or 2 spoonfuls olive oil if needed.) If no electric appliance is available, mince herbs and seasonings and pound in a mortar. Rub herb mixture on lamb.
- Stir together olive oil and lemon juice and paint some generously on meat, reserving remainder. Let meat stand at least 2 hours.
- Preheat oven to 475 degrees. Place leg on rack in roasting pan in center of oven. Lower heat to 350 degrees. Brush meat with reserved oil mixture every 10 minutes.
- Roast until internal temperature at thickest part registers 135 degrees on an instant-read meat thermometer (20 minutes per pound) for rare, 150 degrees for medium, and 165 degrees for medium well-done.
- Let meat rest before slicing across grain.

Greek Meatballs with Mint

Ingredients
- 12 Servings
- 1 lb Ground lean beef
- 1 lb Veal (or pork)
- 2 Eggs
- 1 lg Grated onion
- 1 Tsp Minced fresh mint
- 1 Tsp Oregano
- 2 Tsp Minced fresh parsley
- 2 Minced cloves garlic
- 1 Tsp Tomato paste
- 1 Tablespoon Diluted water
- 2 Tsp Olive oil plus olive oil for pan-frying
- 12 Whole salted wheat crackers and squeezed soaked dry in water
- 1/2 cup Dry white wine salt and freshly Ground pepper to taste flour

Preparation
- Place meat in a large mixing bowl. Break in eggs and mix well. Add onion, mint, oregano, parsley, garlic, diluted tomato paste, the 2 tablespoons oil, crackers, wine, salt, and pepper.

- Knead until well mixed and smooth. On a lightly floured board, shape meat mixture into 12 balls. With your palms, flatten balls into patties, then dust patties lightly with flour.
- In a large skillet over medium heat, warm the remaining oil. Fry patties, turning once, until browned on both sides, 2 to 3 minutes per side or until done to your liking.

Greek Salad

Ingredients
- 1/4 lb Feta cheese cut into 1/2" cubes
- 2 green bell peppers washed and seeded cut into 1" cub
- 1 Cucumber peeled and cut into 1" Cubes
- 3 Tomatoes washed and cut into 1" Cubes
- ½ Sliced stalks celery washed & diagonally
- 1/2 Diced red onion
- 1/2 tsp freshly ground pepper kosher salt
- 3 Tsp Vinegar
- 1/4 cup Oil
- 1/2 tsp Oregano
- 1 Tsp minced fresh basil

Preparation
- In a 2-quart bowl, mix peppers, cucumber, tomatoes, celery, feta cheese, and red onion. Season with salt, pepper, vinegar, oil, oregano, and basil.

Greek Stifado
With Feta Cheese Crust

Ingredients
- 2 Tsp Olive oil
- 3 Tsp Butter
- 3 lb Lean beef stew meat cut into 1" Cubes
- 1 Medium minced onion
- 1/2 cup Tomato paste
- 1/2 cup Dry white wine
- 1/4 cup Red wine vinegar
- 3/4 cup Water
- 2 Tsp Minced garlic

- 1 Bay leaf
- 1 tsp Dried-crumbled oregano leaves
- 1 tsp Ground cinnamon
- 1/2 tsp Ground cumin
- 1/2 tsp Sugar
- 1/4 tsp Cayenne pepper or to taste salt freshly ground black pepper to taste
- 16 Small peeled boiling onions
- 1/2 cup pine nuts
- 1/2 lb Crumbled or grated feta cheese
- 1/2 cup Minced parsley optional hot-pepper sauce

Preparation

- In a large, heavy skillet, heat oil and butter over moderate heat. Raise heat to high and brown meat, one third at a time, removing meat to a large, heavy casserole (preferably with an enamel or porcelain coating) as it browns
- Add minced onion to skillet, sauté just until wilted, and spoon into casserole. Add tomato paste, wine, vinegar, the water, garlic, bay leaf, oregano, cinnamon, cumin, and sugar to the casserole.
- Stir well and add cayenne, salt, and pepper, to taste. Bring just to a boil, cover tightly, lower heat, and simmer 1 hour. Add white boiling onions and simmer, covered, until meat is very tender (about 1 hour longer).
- Degrease stew if necessary and carefully correct seasonings; stir in nuts. Sprinkle feta cheese over stew, pushing it gently into top of liquid with a wooden spoon. Cover and simmer to melt cheese (about 5 minutes longer).
- Sprinkle parsley on top and serve stew in deep soup bowls, making sure that everyone gets some nuts and cheese, but leaving some room in each bowl for rice to be added. Have hot-pepper sauce on hand, to be added as desired.

Greek Walnut Cake

Ingredients

- 1 cup Sugar
- 1 cup Unsalted butter softened plus butter for baking dish
- 6 Eggs
- 1 cup Sifted flour
- 1 cup Farina
- 2 1/2 TB Baking powder
- 1 tsp Ground cinnamon
- 1 tsp Freshly Grated orange zest

- 1 cups Chopped finely walnuts

Preparation

- Prepare syrup and set aside to cool. Preheat oven to 350 degrees. In a large mixing bowl, cream together the 1 cup butter and sugar with a wooden spoon until light and fluffy.
- Add eggs, one at a time, beating continuously. Beat in flour, farina, baking powder, cinnamon, and orange zest. Mix in walnuts. Butter a 9 by 13-inch baking dish and pour batter into it.
- Bake until a knife blade inserted in center comes out clean (about 30 minutes). Remove cake from oven and immediately pour cooled syrup

Grilled/Chilled Tuna With Tangerines

Ingredients
MARINADE
- 1 Tsp Tamari soy sauce
- 1/4 cup Olive oil
- 1 Tsp Chopped fresh fennel leaf
- 2 tsp Fresh celery leaves
- 1/2 tsp Chopped fresh thyme
- 1 small Bay broken leaf
- 2 tsp Grated tangerine zest
- Black pepper

TUNA
- 1 lb fresh tuna center-cut into 4 oz. steaks 1 inch thick
- Tangerines
- Sprigs fresh fennel leaf
- Tangerine and fennel vinaigrette
- 3 Tsp Balsamic vinegar
- 1 tsp Dijon mustard
- 1/2 cup Light olive oil
- 1/2 tsp Grated tangerine zest
- 2 Tsp Fresh fennel leaf
- Salt (or black pepper)

Preparation

- For the marinade, combine all marinade ingredients in a noncreative bowl. Put tuna steaks into marinade and refrigerate 30 min, turning occasionally.
- Break 2 of the tangerines into sections. Squeeze the remaining 2

tangerines, pour juice over sectioned tangerines, and set aside. Heat grill.
- Add mesquite or hickory chips for additional flavor. Remove tuna steaks from marinade and grill over hot fire until fish is just springy to the touch, 1 to 2 minutes per side.
- Tuna should be rare to medium rare. Divide each tuna steak into 3 to 4 slices, cutting against the grain. Drain tangerine sections and reserve juice.
- Arrange tuna slices with drained tangerine sections and fennel sprigs in fan shape on individual plates, cover, and chill.
- Reduce tangerine juice by one-fourth over medium-high heat and use to make vinaigrette. For the vinaigrette, combine vinegar, reduced tangerine juice, and mustard in a noncreative bowl.
- Whisk in oil and season with tangerine zest, chopped fennel leaves, and salt and pepper to taste. Drizzle dressing over arranged salad plates just before serving.

Pork Chops
With Apples in Cider Sauce

Ingredients
- 2 Tsp vegetable oil and approximately to film skillet
- 1/2 lb each Loin pork chops
- 2 Tsp Unsalted butter
- 2 medium Red onions and Peeled Slices cut into 1/4-inch
- 1 Tsp Minced garlic
- 2 lg sweet apples cut into 1/2"
- Slices quartered
- Peeled and cored
- 1 Tsp Fresh sage
- 1 tsp Dried sage
- 1/2 tsp Crumbled dried thyme leaves
- 3/4 cup Unsweetened apple juice
- 1/2 cup Dry white wine
- Salt
- Freshly ground pepper to taste

Preparation
- Film a large, heavy skillet with oil and heat over a high flame until oil is fragrant. Pat pork chops dry, quickly brown on both sides in skillet, and removes to a plate. Lower heat to medium and melt butter in skillet.
- Add onions and sauté, stirring occasionally, until softened. Add garlic and sauté until translucent (1 minute longer).

- Add apples and turn in butter just until completely coated. Return pork chops to skillet, sprinkle with sage and thyme, and add cider and wine.
- Bring liquid to a simmer and cook over fairly low heat until chops are cooked through (20 minutes). With a slotted spatula remove chops and apple mixture from skillet and keep warm.
- Reduce cooking liquid at a full boil over high flame, stirring constantly, until it has thickened to the consistency of light syrup. Add salt and pepper to taste, pour liquid over chops and apples, and serve hot.

Roasted Chicken
(With Lemon-Parsley Sauce)

Ingredients
- Lemon
- 4 Tsp Butter
- Whole split chicken breasts
- Salt
- Fresh Ground black pepper
- 1/3 cup Chopped parsley

Preparation
- Heat oven to 450F. Squeeze 1/4 cup lemon juice. Melt the butter in a small saucepan or in the microwave. Sprinkle chicken with salt and pepper.
- Put chicken in a baking dish skin side up and drizzle with half of the butter. Bake until skin is crisp and golden brown and juices run clear, about 25 to 30 minutes.
- Put chicken on a serving platter and keep warm. Stir the lemon juice and remaining butter into pan juices, scraping the pan with a wooden spoon to deglaze.
- Add the parsley and season to taste with salt and pepper. Pour sauce over chicken and serve immediately.

Stuffed Grape Leaves

Ingredients
- 1/4 cup Dried currants
- 1 cup Dry white wine
- 12 Tsp Olive oil
- Chopped green onions and green tops
- 1 Tsp Minced fresh parsley

- 1/4 cup Pine nuts
- Salt
- Freshly Ground pepper to taste
- 16 oz Boiling grape leaves preserved in brine water
- 6 Tsp Fresh lemon juice
- 2 cups Beef stock
- Lemon wedges & chilled plain
- Yogurt for accompaniment

Preparation

- In a small bowl combine currants and wine; set aside. In a small skillet over medium heat, warm 2 tablespoons of the oil. Add onions and parsley and sauté until onions are translucent (about 5)
- Add rice, dill, pine nuts, currants and wine, salt, and pepper; stir to mix, cover, and simmer until liquid is absorbed (about 10 minutes). Remove from heat and cool.
- Remove grape leaves from jar and immerse in boiling water about 30 seconds; drain and rinse under cold water. Cut off and discard tough stems.
- Pat leaves dry with paper towels, then place shiny side down on a flat surface, place a rounded teaspoon of the rice mixture on center of each leaf.
- Fold base end of leaf over filling to cover; fold in sides of leaf, overlapping them, then roll up carefully to form a sealed cylinder about 2 inches long.
- Repeat with remaining leaves. In bottom of a Dutch oven or other heavy, broad-bottomed pan, arrange a layer of stuffed leaves, seam side down, close together.
- Sprinkle with some of the lemon juice and 2 tablespoons of the olive oil. Repeat, making as many layers as necessary to accommodate all of the stuffed leaves; sprinkle each layer with lemon juice and olive oil.
- Our in beef stock and the remaining olive oil, being careful not to disturb layers. Place a heavy plate on top to weight down stuffed leaves.
- Cover and simmer over very low heat until rice is tender (about 40 minutes). To test, open one of the packets. Remove from heat and lift stuffed leaves out with a slotted utensil.

Whole Stuffed Leg of Lamb

Ingredients
STUFFING:
- 2 cups Cooked al dente bulgur
- Minced cloves garlic

- 1 lg Chopped onion
- Chopped stalks celery
- 1 Chopped bell pepper and seeded
- Small Minced fresh hot chilies, seeded
- 1/3 cup Minced fresh parsley
- 1 Tsp Minced fresh dill weed
- 1 tsp Dried dill weed
- 1/2 tsp Ground cumin
- Tsp Fresh lemon juice
- 1 tsp Grated lemon peel
- Bay leaf
- 1/3 cup Pine nuts
- 1/3 cup Currants
- Lightly beaten eggs
- 1 tsp Sugar
- Salt
- Coarsely Ground black pepper to taste
- lb Leg of lamb
- Marinade
- Fresh lemon juice
- 1/4 cup Sugar
- 1/4 cup Olive oil
- 1 Tsp Minced fresh dill weed
- Finely minced cloves garlic
- 1/4 tsp Cayenne
- 1 tsp Dry mustard
- 1/2 tsp mixed dried herbs Italian-seasoning
- 1/2 Tsp Paprika
- Fresh Ground black pepper
- 1/2 cup Beef broth
- Lettuce leaves
- Tomato-wedges
- Lemon Slices (optional)

Preparation
- Combine all of the ingredients for the stuffing and pack them firmly into the leg of lamb. Truss shut with bamboo or metal skewers.
- Mix all the ingredients for the marinade together exceedingly well. Put the stuffed leg of lamb in a deep dish, pour the marinade over, and rub it into the meat on all sides.
- Refrigerate overnight, turning and rubbing several times. To bake, place the lamb in a roasting pan with a tight fitting lid.
- Mix the broth with the remaining marinade and pour over the leg of lamb, bake at 350 degrees for 1 1/2 hours or until the meat is exceedingly tender.

- Remove lid during last 20 minutes, turn the heat to 400 degrees to brown.

Part 7: India Recipes

The cuisine of India is characterized by the use of various, spices ,herbs, and other vegetables and also for the widespread practice of vegetarianism across many sections of its society. Each family of Indian cuisine represents a wide assortment of dishes and cooking techniques. As a consequence, it varies from region to region. India's religious beliefs and culture have also played an influential role in the evolution of its cuisine.

Bedvi
(Indian Snack)

Ingredients
- 1 cup Semolina
- ½ cup Sieved flour
- 1 ½ tsp Salt
- ¾ cup Water
- ½ cup Washed lentils
- 1 tbsp Chopped ginger
- 2 tsp Chopped green chilies
- A pinch of onion seeds
- A pinch of asafetida powder
- A pinch of garam masala
- ½ tsp Vegetable soda
- 4 tsp Oil for frying

Preparation
- Pick, wash and soak the lentils in water for 45 minutes.
- Mix the flour, salt and semolina together. Add water and make a medium strong dough. Roughly flatten the dough with wet finger tips and divide into 16 equal parts.
- For the filling, grind the drained lentils, ginger and green chilies to a paste. Add onion seeds, asafetida, garam masala a soda powder. Divide into 16 equal parts.
- Flatten one part of dough and place one part of the filling in it. Shape into a ball.
- Roll out each ball to a diameter of 5cm, using oil to avoid from sticking.
- Deep fry in hot oil till golden brown. Drain excess oil and serve hot.

Bhakar Wadi

Ingredients
- 240 g. Gram flour
- 120 g. Wheat flour
- Salt to taste
- A pinch of asafoetida
- Oil for deep frying
- 100 g. Grated coconut
- 60 g. Sesame seeds

- 60 g. Poppy seeds
- A pinch of sugar
- Salt and chili powder to taste
- 100 g. Coriander leaves, chopped fine
- A marble sized ball of tamarind, soaked in a little water
- Black masala powder (branded curry powder) to taste

Preparation

- Mix together gram flour and wheat flour.
- Add salt, asafoetida, 60 ml. hot oil and enough water.
- Knead to a stiff dough. Keep it aside.
- Roast the grated coconut, sesame seeds and poppy seeds and grind to a powder.
- Add sugar, salt, chili powder and coriander leaves to the masala powder to prepare the filling for bhakar wadi.
- Add tamarind pulp and black masala powder and mix well.
- Divide the dough into small portions and roll each portion into a thin rectangular shaped chappati.
- Spread the filling all over the chappati and roll up the dough with the filling into a tight cylindrical shape.
- Seal the edges with a little water.
- Cut into three cm. long pieces and deep fry in hot oil till brown and crisp.
- Remove from oil and store in an airtight container.

Bhel

Ingredients

- 1 1/2 cups Puffed rice
- 1 Onion
- 1 Tomato
- 1 Small boiled peeled potato
- 1/2 tbsp Coriander leaves
- 1/2 cup Fine sev
- 1/4 cup Parboiled moong sprouts -- optional
- 1 tsp Roasted peanuts -- optional
- 1 tsp Hot green chutney
- 1 1/2 tsp Tamarind chutney
- Salt to taste
- 1/4 Lime juice
- 10-12 Puries (used for bhel or panipuri optional) crushed

Preparation
- Just before serving. In a large mixing bowl, add puffed rice, and all ingredients except 1/4 the coriander and sev. Mix well.
- Sprinkle a few drops water if too dry. Adjust taste and salt.
- Spoon into individual bowls. Sprinkle some sev and coriander to garnish.
- Serve immediately.

Samosa

Ingredients
COVER:
- 1 cup Plain flour (maida)
- 2 tbsp. Warm oil
- Water to knead dough

FILLING:
- 2 Large boiled, peeled, mashed potatoes
- 1 Finely chopped onion
- 2 Green chilies crushed
- 1/2 tsp. Ginger crushed
- 1/2 tsp. Garlic crushed
- 1 tbsp. Coriander finely chopped
- 1/2 Lemon juice extracted
- 1/2 tsp. Turmeric powder
- 1/2 tsp. Garam masala
- 1/2 tsp. Coriander seeds cru shed
- 1 tsp. Red chili powder
- Salt to taste
- Oil to deep fry

Preparation (for dough)
- Make well in the flour.
- Add oil, salt and little water. Mix well till crumbly.
- Add more water little by little, kneading into soft pliable dough.
- Cover with moist cloth, keep aside for 15-20 minutes.
- Beat dough on work surface and knead again. Re-cover.

Preparation (for filling)
- Heat 3 tbsp. oil, add ginger, green chili, garlic, coriander seeds.
- Stir fry for a minute, add onion, sauté till light brown.

- Add coriander, lemon, turmeric, salt, red chili, garam masala.
- Stir fry for 2 minutes, add potatoes. Stir further 2 minutes. Cool. Keep aside.

Preparation (for Samosa)
- Make a thin 5" diameter. round with some dough.
- Cut into two halves. Run a moist finger along diameter.
- Join and press together to make a cone.
- Place a tbsp. of filling in the cone and seal third side as above.
- Make five to six. Put in hot oil, deep fry on low to medium till light brown.
- Do not fry on high, or the samosas will turn out oily and soggy.
- Drain on rack or kitchen paper.
- Serve hot with green and tamarind chutneys, or tomato sauce.

Simple Potato Cake

Ingredients
- 3 Large potatoes
- 1 Capsicum
- 1/2 cup Grated cheese
- 1/2 cup Bread crumbs
- 1/2 cup Milk
- 1 red Chili crushed
- 2 tsp Butter
- 1 tbsp. Plain flour

Preparation
- The potatoes will turn out best if boiled and refrigerated overnight before using.
- Do not peel potatoes. Slice into thin rounds or grate coarsely.
- Deseed capsicum and slice into thin rounds
- Heat a thick nonstick pan about 5" diameter.
- Meanwhile mix cheese, milk, crumbs, flour and chili.
- If mixture feels thin, add some more bread crumbs.
- Add salt to taste. Apply 1 tsp. on bottom of pan.
- Arrange potatoes to cover the pan. Top with capsicum.
- Pour the mixture all over evenly. Level to cover all the potatoes.
- Sprinkle fresh ground pepper, salt and simmer on low till bottom is golden brown.
- Flip over very carefully with a wide sharp spatula, and roast the other side.

- Let in the remaining butter around the edges to seep down.
- Let other side become golden brown too.
- Flip on serving plate and make sections with a knife.
- Serve hot and crisp.
- Variation: Bake the same if desired, instead if roasting.
Making time: 40 minutes

Spiced Chick Peas

Ingredients
- ½ kg Boiled and drained chick peas
- 1 tsp Garam masala
- 2 tsp Lemon juice
- 1 Chopped green chili,
- 1 Chopped small onion
- 1 Chopped small tomato
- 2 Sprigs of parsley
- Salt to taste

Preparation
- Heat oil in saucepan. Add peas.
- Sauté for a minute and add all the ingredients, mixing thoroughly.
- Cook for 2 more minutes before serving.
- Garnish with parsley and quartered tomato and onion rings.

Tandoori Potatoes

Ingredients
- 1 tsp Lemon juice
- 1 tbsp Chopped cashew nuts
- 2 tsp Raisins
- 2 tsp Clarified butter (ghee)
- 4 tsp Cottage cheese (paneer), grated
- ½ tsp Chaat Masala 1 kg Peeled potatoes (large)
- Oil for frying
- Salt to taste
- 1 tsp Red chili powder
- A pinch garam masala

Preparation

- Scoop out the centers of the potatoes. Deep fry shells and centers separately till the sides become crisp. Allow centers to cool and mash.
- Mix together mashed potatoes, salt, red chili, garam masala, lemon juice, cashew nuts, raisings and clarified butter. Fill the potato cases with this and top up with cottage cheese.
- Skewer 4 pieces each, per skewer and grill till golden brown in color.
- Sprinkle chaat masala and serve hot, garnished with chopped coriander.

Vegetable Pie

Ingredients

- 2 cups Plain flour (maida)
- 100 gms. Chilled butter
- 1/2 tsp. Salt
- Chilled water

FILLING:

- 2 cups Chopped vegetables of choice (eg., potatoes, peas, beans, carrot, spinach, cauliflower etc, All or any)
- 2 Onions
- 1 Tomato
- 2 Green chilies
- 1/2" Piece ginger
- 1 tbsp. Oil
- 1/2 tsp. Red chili powder
- 1/2 tsp. Curry masala (or garam masala)
- 1 tbsp. Cream
- 1 tsp. Corn flour
- Salt to taste

Preparation

- Sieve together flour and salt.
- Add chilled butter. Mix with fork till mixture is crumbly. Sprinkle chilled water over it.
- Quickly, with light hand mix the dough into a lump. Do not over knead.
- Chill dough for 15 min. in a plastic bag.
- Roll dough into 4" thick round.
- Place over a greased pie plate.
- Prick with a fork all over.
- Bake in a pre-heated oven for 12 min., or till light brown. Keep aside.
- For Filling: Grate tomato, onion, ginger. Finely chop green chilies.

- Chop and boil other vegetables.
- Heat oil in a skillet, add the grated vegetables and chilies. Cook for 4-5 mins. Stirring occasionally.
- Add all other ingredients except cream. Cook till the water evaporates and curry is thick.
- Sprinkle a little corn flour over the crust.
- Pour and spread the filling in the shell. Pour cream all over.
- Bake for 8-10 mins. in pre-heated oven.
- Slice and serve warm.

Meat or Chicken Kurma Curry

Ingredients
- 2 lb. Meat / Chicken
- 60g Alagappa's Kurma Curry Powder
- 1 cup Thick coconut milk
- 2 cups thin coconut milk (both thick and thin extracted from 1 grated coconut)
- Few mint leaves
- 1 cup of Water
- Cooking oil
- Salt to taste

Seasoning A: (spices to grind)
- 7 Shallots
- 4 Garlic cloves
- 5cm Ginger knob
- 3 Green chilies
- 1 tbsp Cashew nuts
- 5 Blanched almonds

Seasoning B:
- 2 Star anise
- 4 Cardamoms
- 5cm Cinnamon stick
- 3 Cloves
- 2 Medium size sliced onion

Preparation
- Heat oil in pan, sauté Seasoning B till slightly golden brown. Put meat / chicken, salt and water, stir fry for 15 minutes Add ground Seasoning A and Alagappa's Kurma Curry Powder.
- Toss in thin coconut milk, bring to boil and then toss in thick coconut milk. Simmer over low heat until gravy is thickened. Add mint leaves and

- serve while hot.
- Note: If required gravy thin, add 2 cups of water.

Chicken Curry (Spicy)

Ingredients

- For the marinade:
- 4 Skinned Chicken (350g each)
- 4 tsp Ginger paste
- 4 tsp Garlic paste
- 1 tsp Red chili powder
- 1/3 tsp Turmeric powder
- Salt to taste
- For the filling:
- 200 gm Minced chicken
- 2 tbsp Sautéed onions
- 2 tsp finely chopped ginger
- ½ tsp Crushed peppercorns
- A pinch of black cumin
- 4 Green cardamom
- ½ tsp Coriander powder
- 1/3 tsp Fennel powder
- 10 Finely chopped almonds
- 20 pistachios, chopped finely
- 1 Finely chopped cashew nut
- For the curry:
- 1 ½ cup Yogurt
- 1 tsp Red chili powder
- Salt to taste
- 5 tsp Almond paste
- 1/3 tsp Mace) javitri) powder
- 5 Green cardamoms
- 4 tbsp Butter

Preparation

- Clean the chicken, marinate with ginger-garlic pastes, red chili, turmeric and salt for 4 hours. For the filling, mix all the ingredients and divide into 4 parts. Stuff the stomach cavity of each chicken with one portion of filling.
- Skewer the chickens and roast in a tandoor or in a very hot oven for 8-10 minutes. Whisk together all the ingredients for the curry. Place the chicken in a handi (pot) or an oven-proof dish, along with the yogurt mixture and

cook on low heat for 25 to 30 minutes.
- Serve hot, accompanied by an Indian bread.

Tandoori Chicken

Ingredients
- 12 pieces of Chicken (drum sticks or thighs)
- 1/2 cup Tandoori chicken powder.
- 1/2 cup Plain yogurt
- Salt as required
- 2 Lime
- One whole white onion
- One green and one red bell-pepper (optional)
- Flat aluminum tray (and foil)

Preparation
- Skin the chicken pieces and make 3-4 deep cuts on each one of them. Mix yogurt, tandoori powder, mustard oil and salt as required. Mix the paste with chicken pieces and let it stand for at least 6 hours.
- After marinating is done, arrange pieces in tray, cover with foil bake at 350 F for 20 minutes. Reduce heat to 250 F, and then bake and broil alternately in 30 min. cycles for 2 hrs.
- Occasionally, take the tray, out, and rearrange the chicken pieces before putting them back in. If there is too much water inside, drain the water. If the chicken pieces look too dry, sprinkle some water mixed with lime juice on them.
- After baking is done, take the pieces out and brush off the excess tandoori paste from them. Put the pieces in an open tray in the oven for 2-3 minutes (just to get them look crisp and dry.)
- You can add a garnishing of stir-fried onions and bell-peppers and lime juice on the chicken before serving. It should be served hot.

Lime Pickle

Ingredients
- Fresh lime (large size, thin skin, ripe) - 6
- 4 spoons Salt
- 2 spoon Red chili powder
- 1/2 spoon Asafoetida
- 1/4 cup of Sesame oil

- Mustard seeds
- 4 Spoons of oil
- Fenugreek seeds
- Asafetida

Preparation
- Cut fresh limes into medium pieces. (Preserve the juice while cutting). Add salt, red chili powder, asafoetida and mix well. Next day add sesame oil and leave it aside. Next day, add mustard seeds to oil and when it splatters add fenugreek seeds and asafoetida.
- Add this to the pickle and mix. Store in refrigerator.

Cheese Ice-cream

Ingredients
- 1 liter Milk
- 50 gm Home-made cottage cheese
- ¼ cup Powdered sugar
- 4-5 Powdered cardamoms

Preparation
- Boil milk until it reduces to half its volume. Add sugar, cardamom powder and bring to boil again, stirring constantly. Add cottage cheese. Stir well. When mixture thickens a little, remove from heat.
- Transfer to a baking tin and cool. Place tin in freezer, covered with foil or plastic wrap, to set.

Double Ka Meetha
(Bread Pudding)

Ingredients
- 1 Loaf bread (small)
- 1 liter Milk
- 500 gms Sugar
- 250 gms Double cream
- 250 gms Clarified butter
- 100 gms Chopped and roasted cashew nuts
- 100 gms Almonds (soaked and chopped fine)
- 10 gm Saffron
- 5 Cardamom powdered

Preparation

- Cut each bread slice into four pieces. Fry them in clarified butter till golden brown.
- Make a sugar syrup by adding half a litre of water to the sugar and boil it for 15 minutes.
- Add the powdered cardamom and the saffron dissolved in milk to the sugar syrup.
- Boil milk until it is thickened.
- Arrange the fried bread pieces on a flat tray and sprinkle the chopped nuts on them.
- Pour the sugar syrup, double cream and milk alternately over the bread pieces while they are still hot.
- Refrigerate and serve as dessert.

Indian Fruit Dip

Ingredients

- 1 (8 oz) glass of cream cheese
- ¼ cup orange juice
- ¼ cup icing sugar
- ½ tsp rose essence
- 1 cup fresh cream

Preparation

- Beat all ingredients until blended well.
- Serve with a fruit plate.

Indian Vermicelli Pudding

Ingredients

- 2 cups wheat vermicelli
- 2 liters milk
- 2 crushed cardamoms
- 200 gm sugar
- 4 tbsp vegetable fat
- Pistachios or almonds for garnishing

Preparation:

- Heat fat in a large pan.
- Stir fry vermicelli until golden brown and set aside.

- Boil milk in a heavy pan and add vermicelli.
- Simmer on low heat for 10 minutes, stirring regularly.
- When the milk and vermicelli thicken, add sugar and cook for few more minutes until mixture thickens to a creamy consistency.
- Remove from heat, add crushed cardamoms and let the pudding cook.
- Place in refrigerator until cold and garnish with pistachios or almonds.
- This pudding can also be served hot.

Nankhatais
(Indian cookies)

Ingredients:
- 150 gm flour
- 100 gm ghee or clarified butter
- 115 gm fine sugar
- 1/8 tsp baking powder
- ¼ cup milk
- 5 powdered cardamoms
- Rose essence
- Blanched, chopped almonds or pistachios

Preparation
- Sift flour and baking powder. Add sugar mix well.
- Work in ghee, cardamom powder and essence.
- Add milk and knead to a soft dough.
- Shape dough into small balls, press gently.
- Garnish with chopped almonds or pistachios and bake in preheated moderate oven (180 degrees C) for 20 minutes or until golden brow

Eggs in Coconut Milk

Ingredients
- 6 hard-boiled eggs
- 1 minced clove garlic
- 1 small sliced onion
- 1 tablespoon oil
- 1/2 teaspoon salt
- pepper to taste
- 1 tablespoon curry powder

- 1 cup coconut milk
- 1 small sweet pepper

Preparation

- Peel the hard-boiled eggs and cut into quarters.
- Fry onion and garlic in oil until golden.
- Add the curry powder, salt, and peppers.
- Mix well and gradually add the coconut milk and then the chopped sweet peppers.
- Cook until it thickens.
- Remove from heat and add the cooked eggs.

Stuffed Eggs

Ingredients

- 4 hard-boiled eggs
- 1/4 cup grated cheese
- 1/2 cup meat (cooked and minced)
- 1 chopped finely onion
- 2 tbsp sour cream
- 1 tbsp tomato sauce
- 2 chopped finely green chilies
- 1/4 cup bread crumbs
- 1 tbsp butter
- salt to taste
- 2 tbsp chopped finely coriander leaves

Preparation

- Peel the eggs. Halve the eggs (lengthwise). Remove the yolks in a vessel.
- Mix cheese, green chilies, onion, meat, salt, coriander leaves, salt, tomato sauce, sour cream.
- Grease the baking dish with the butter.
- Stuff the egg whites with the mixture and place it on baking dish.
- Garnish the stuffed egg with bread crumbs.
- Place the dish in pre-heated moderated oven for 7 minutes or till golden brown on top. Serve hot.

Fish Curry

Ingredients
- 1/2 kg White fish fillet
- 1 Chopped onions
- 1 Grinded onions
- 1 tsp each of Ginger-Garlic paste
- 3 tbsp Tomato puree
- 1/2 cup Water
- 1/2 cup Ghee
- 1 tsp White cumin seeds
- 1 tsp Turmeric powder
- 1 tsp Garam masala powder
- Salt To Taste

Preparation
- Cut the fish into medium-sized pieces.
- Heat the ghee in a pan and fry the fish pieces gently until light brown.
- Add the chopped onion to the ghee in the pan and fry until golden.
- Add White cumin seeds, turmeric, garam masala and cook stirring for few seconds.
- Now add the grinded onion, garlic, ginger and tomato puree.
- Fry the mixture until the ghee starts to separate.
- Add the water and salt and bring the mixture to the boil.
- Add fried fish pieces, reduce the heat and simmer for about 10 minutes.
- Enjoy hot Fish Curry with rice or roti.

Sultanpuri Pilau

Ingredients:
- 1 1/2 cups long grain rice
- 750 g (1 1/2 lb) lamb forequarter chops
- 4 cups water
- 1 small onion, chopped
- 2 cardamom pods, lightly bruised
- 2 bay leaves
- Small piece cinnamon stick
- 2 1/2 teaspoons salt
- 1/2 cup milk
- 1 tablespoon ghee

- 2 tablespoons oil
- 1 large onion, finely sliced
- 1 tablespoon finely shredded fresh ginger
- 2 teaspoons finely sliced garlic
- 1/2 teaspoon black cummi seeds
- 2 fresh red chilies, seeded and sliced
- 1/8 teaspoon saffron strands or pinch powdered saffron
- Pinch red coloring powder

Preparation

- Wash rice well and leave to drain.
- Put lamb into a large saucepan with water, the chopped onion, cardamom pods, bay leaves, cinnamon stick and salt.
- Bring to the boil, then skim surface, cover and simmer gently for at least 1 hour until meat is tender.
- Remove meat from pan and leave until cool enough to handle.
- Measure stock. If more than 2 1/2 cups continue cooking with lid off pan until it is reduced to this amount.
- Add milk to make 3 cups.
- Cut meat into cubes, discarding bones and fat.
- Heat ghee and oil in a large, heavy saucepan and fry the finely sliced onion until soft.
- Add ginger and garlic and continue frying and stirring frequently until they are golden. Remove to a plate.
- Add meat to pan and fry, stirring, until meat is browned, remove with slotted spoon and set aside with the fried onion mixture.
- Fry the black cumin seeds and the chilies for 1 minute and set aside separately.
- Put half the washed and drained rice into the saucepan and spread with the meat and onion mixture, then cover with remaining rice.
- Sprinkle the black cumin seeds and chilies over rice.
- Reserve 1 tablespoon of milk and stock and gently pour the stock over the rice.
- Bring to the boil, then turn heat very low, cover tightly and allow to cook for 20 minutes.
- Meanwhile, heat the reserved stock and dissolve the saffron in it.
- If saffron strands are used, pound them first in mortar and pestle. If powdered saffron is used, put it straight into the hot stock.
- Add a very little red coloring also to give a bright orange-red color.
- When the rice has cooked for 20 minutes, pour the saffron liquid over the top. It will not color many grains, but this is the way it should be.
- Replace the lid and leave for a further 5 minutes.
- Before serving, gently fork the colored grains through the rice. Serve hot.

Biryani

Ingredients

- 2 lbs Spring Lamb (cleaned and cut into medium size pieces)
- 4 oz. Yogurt
- 4 ozs Ghee
- 1 lb Rice (washed)
- 4 ozs Onions (sliced finely)
- 1 oz Ginger & Garlic (equal amounts crushed)
- 1 Lemon
- 1 oz Almonds (ground)
- 2 Cinnamon sticks
- 4-6 Cardamoms
- 1 oz Milk
- 1/4 tsp Safron
- 2-3 Green Chilies
- 1/2 tsp Black Zeera
- 2-3 Cloves
- 1/2 tsp Garam Masala (equal amounts of Black Zeera, Cardamons & Cinnamon sticks, with half amount of cloves)
- Salt to taste
- Coriander and Fried Onions to Garnish

Preparation

- In a large bowl mix the meat, yogurt, almonds, chopped green chilies, ginger and garlic, salt, and ground garam masala.
- To the mixture add half a teaspoon each of chili powder and turmeric. Marinate for at least 4-6 hours in the fridge.
- Fry the onions in ghee until golden brown and crisp. Drain away any excess ghee and then remove the onions and spread over a large plate. This should keep the onions crispy.
- Once they have cooled crush the onions with your fingers and add this to the marinated meat mixture.
- In a large pan half fill with water and add salt, whole garam masala and one green chili.
- Bring this to the boil and add the washed rice and cook until the water boils.
- Once the water has boiled drain the rice in a colander and rinse with a little cold water.
- Grease the saucepan generously with ghee and transfer the meat mixture.
- Level the surface and now spread the rice evenly over the meat.

- Squeeze the lemon and pour the juice over the rice.
- Warm the milk and crush the safron into it.
- Pour the milk/safron mixture over the rice. Dot generously with ghee.
- To garnish spread the fried onions and corriander over the rice.
- Cover the saucepan tightly. Allow to steam on high heat for about 10 minutes and then lower the heat and cook for another 1 and a half to 2 hours.
- Before removing the pan from the cooker ensure that there is no moisture left in the meat. This can be checked by simply listening for a sizzling sound. If there is no sizzling then the Biryani is ready.
- Biryani is traditionally served with Mirch Salan and Yoghurt Chutney.

Exotic Chicken Biryani

Ingredients
- 1 kg chicken, cleaned, cut into 8 pieces
- 2 ½ cups rice, basmati or any long grain variety
- 3 cups yogurt, whisked
- 0.5 gm saffron, dissolve in milk
- ½ cup milk
- ¼ cup cream
- 2 tsp mint leaves, chopped
- 2 tsp green coriander, chopped
- 4 liters water
- 2 bay leaves
- 10 green cardamoms
- 10 cloves
- Salt to taste
- 2 black cardamoms
- 4 cinnamon sticks
- 1 1/3 tsp black cumin seeds
- ½ cup onions, sliced
- 2 2/3 tbsp ginger paste
- 2 2/3 tbsp garlic paste
- 2 tsp lemon juice
- ¾ cup butter, unsalted
- 1 tsp mace powder
- 2 tsp red chili powder

Preparation
- Wash the rice and soak it for at least half an hour.
- Divide yogurt in 2 equal portions. Add saffron milk and cream to 1 portion

- along with mint and coriander. Keep aside.
- Preheat the oven to 150 degrees C.
- Boil water (4 liters) in a large pan and add one bay leaf, 2 green cardamoms and 2 cloves. Add the rice and salt to taste, boil for a few minutes until the rice is half cooked.
- Drain the rice with the whole spices and keep aside.
- Heat butter in a pan, add the remaining whole spices and black cumin, sauté over medium heat until the cumin begins to crackle. Add onions and sauté until golden brown. Add ginger-garlic pastes and red chilies, stir for 15 seconds. Add the chicken and salt to taste, cook further for 3-4 minutes.
- Add the second portion of plain yogurt along with water (200 ml), bring to a boil, lower heat and simmer until the chicken is almost done. Stir in lemon juice.
- Grease a large baking dish, spread half the chicken, sprinkle half of the saffron-yogurt mixture on top, cover with half of the rice. Repeat the layering process and place a moist cloth over the final layer. Cover the dish and seal with dough.
- Bake in slow oven for 20 to 25 minutes. Remove and serve hot, garnished with fried almonds and accompanied by Boondi Raita.

Indian Rice

Ingredients
- 3 cups Basmati, Indian long grain rice, washed and soaked for half an hour
- 1 cup peas
- 1 onion finely chopped
- 1 tsp garlic-ginger paste
- 1 big carrot, grated
- 1 tsp salt
- 1 bay leaf
- 2 cardamoms, crushed
- 4 cloves
- 1 thumb-sized cinnamon stick
- 1 tsp lemon juice
- 4 tbsp oil
- 3 tbsp clarified butter of ghee
- 100 gm chopped nuts, cherries, raisins and pineapple bits for garnishing

Preparation
- Heat oil and plunge all spices. When brown, add chopped onions and fry until soft and transparent.
- Add grated carrot, peas, ginger-garlic paste and fry for one minute, stirring constantly.

- Stir in rice, then add water and lemon juice.
- Bring to boil, then simmer for 20 minutes, covered loosely over tiny flame.
- Turn cooked Indian rice or biryani onto serving plate.
- Remove bay leaf, cloves and cinnamon stick.
- Melt butter in a saucepan and pour hot melted butter over the rice dish.
- Sprinkle nuts, raisins and pineapple bits on top.
- Enjoy your Indian Rice. Hope you love this Indian recipe.

Onion Rice

Ingredients

- 1 cup rice.
- 1 medium sized onion.
- 1/2 cup green peas.
- 3 minced green chilies.
- A little garlic.
- Mustard and cumin seeds for seasoning.
- cut coriander leaves.
- salt to taste.

Preparation

- Cut onions into thin long slices.
- Boil the rice separately.
- Heat oil in a pan and season with mustard and cumin seeds.
- Add cut onions and green chilies , fry until onion is light brown in color and add green peas. Pour little water and allow the mixture to boil till the mixture is dry.
- Add the boiled rice and coriander leaves into the mixture and mix well.

Saffron Rice

Ingredients

- 1 ½ cup long grain rice
- 2 tbsp vegetable oil
- 1 (3 inch) cinnamon stick
- 7 whole cloves
- 5 cardamom pods (optional)

- 1 tsp salt
- ¼ tsp crumbled saffron
- 2 tsp milk
- 2 ¾ cup water

Preparation

- Rinse rice.
- In a saucepan, heat oil.
- Add cinnamon, cloves and cardamom pods.
- Fry the spices, stirring for 30 seconds.
- Add rice, stir for a minute.
- Add water and salt, bring to boil.
- Cover and cook over low heat for 15 minutes.
- Add milk to saffron and cook until hot, dribble over rice and continue to cook rice for 5 minutes.
- Remove from heat. Let stand for 5 minutes.

Coconut Prawn Gravy

Ingredients

- 750 gms Prawns
- 1 large Onions, ground to a paste
- 2 medium Onions, sliced finely
- 2 tbsp Chili paste
- 2 Bay leaves
- 1 cup thick Coconut Milk
- 1 cup thin (milk can be extracted from one large coconut, or tinned coconut milk may also be used)
- 2 to 5 Green Cardamom
- Salt to taste
- Oil for frying

Preparation

- Wash and dry the prawns in a kitchen towel. Set aside.
- Heat oil in a wok (kadai). Add bay leaves and green cardamom and fry for a few minutes.
- Add sliced onions and fry till golden brown. Then add the ground onion paste and the chili paste.
- Fry for several minutes adding little water, as necessary, to prevent the masala from burning.
- Add the prawns. Stir thoroughly and then add the thin coconut milk.
- Keep simmering in high heat till the gravy reduces to a half. Add salt to

taste.
- Finally add thick coconut milk and simmer in medium heat for 12 to 15 minutes.
- Serve hot with rice.

Crab Curry

Ingredients
- 1/2 kg crab
- 4 kashmiri red chilies
- 2 tbsp coriander
- ½ tbsp turmeric 11
- 4 pods garlic
- ginger, small piece
- 1/4 tbsp cumin
- 1 big onion
- 1 big tomatoes
- coconut, as per taste
- tamarind juice, little as per taste. (if more then it will be more sour.)
- salt to taste

Preparation
- Cut the crab 4 pieces (or as per taste)
- Grind ginger, garlic, chilies, coriander, coconut, cumin into thick paste.
- In a kadhai, add oil, put mustard , then add cut onion, fry well.
- Add tomatoes and fry well.
- Then add the masala and fry well till oil leaves.
- Add the crabs and boil well.
- Add tamarind juice and cook for 10 minutes.
- Garnish with cilantro.

###

Part 8: Irish Recipes

Irish food is known for the quality and freshness of its ingredients. Most cooking is done without herbs or spices, except for salt and pepper. Foods are usually served without sauce or gravy.

The staples of the Irish diet have traditionally been potatoes, grains (especially oats), and dairy products. Potatoes still appear at most Irish meals, with potato scones, similar to biscuits or muffins, a specialty in the north. The Irish have also been accomplished cheese makers for centuries. Ireland makes about fifty types of homemade "farmhouse" cheeses, which are considered delicacies.

Ardshane House Irish Stew

Ingredients
- 4 lb Cut in Middle neck of lamb one inch chunks
- 4 lb Peeled Potatoes
- 10 small sliced Onions
- 2 oz Pearl barley
- 2 pt Beef stock
- To Taste Salt and pepper

Preparation
- That's the basic recipe. You can add a load of sliced carrots and leeks to make it go further and about 5-6 tsps of Worchester shire sauce or regular brown sauce "wot you Yanks pour over everything!!"
- If you like, you could add a half a pint of Guinness to your stock. I make my stock from the potato peelings, carrot tops, leek ends, and any other stuff I find lurking in the refrigerator.
- If you chuck in a few moldy lamb bones and boil/simmer for several hours, you should get a damned good stock (strain the liquid or you'll get God knows what stuck in your teeth!!) You'll need to start with about 5 pints of liquid.
- Then bung everything into a ginormous pan, bring to the boil, and then simmer for about two hours...should taste bloody orgasmic! Salt and pepper to taste, depending on your level of drunkeness!!"

Baby Carrots and Onions in Cream

Ingredients
- 1 lb Baby carrots
- 1 lb Small white onions
- 5 fl Cream
- 1 Salt and pepper
- Pinch nutmeg

Preparation

- Wash and trim carrots. Peel onions. Place in pot with 1/2 inch boiling salted water. Cover and simmer gently for 10 minutes.
- Remove lid and boil rapidly, shaking pot to prevent burning, until water is absorbed. Stir in cream and add pepper and salt to taste, if necessary. Serve with a very light sprinkling of nutmeg.

Baked Parsnips Irish Style

Ingredients

- 1/2 lb Parsnips
- 2 oz Butter (or bacon fat)
- 3 T Stock
- 1 Salt and pepper
- Pinch nutmeg

Preparation

- Peel parsnips, quarter, and remove any woody core. Parboil for 15 minutes. Place in an ovenproof dish. Add stock and sprinkle with salt, pepper and nutmeg.
- Dot with butter and bake for 30 minutes on a low shelf in a moderate oven. (Generally parsnips are baked in the same oven as the main meat dish, whose cooking temperature governs that of the parsnips.)

Irish Sausages

Ingredients

- 1 1/2 lb Lean pork
- 8 oz without gristle Pork fat
- 1/2 tsp Ground allspice
- 1 tsp Salt
- Fresh-ground pepper
- Pinch sage (or marjoram) Dried
- 1 oz White breadcrumbs (optional)
- Ground ginger and mace nutmeg cloves
- Cayenne pepper

Preparation

- Mince the meat and fat twice, then mix very well and season. (Fry a teaspoon or so each time to check the flavor until you get it the way you

like it.)
- Add the herbs and breadcrumbs and any spices used. Fill skins as usual.

Black Pudding (Irish)

Ingredients
- 1 tsp Salt
- 1 lb Pig's liver
- 1 1/2 lb Chopped unrendered lard
- 120 fl Pig's blood
- 2 lb Breadcrumbs
- 4 oz Oatmeal
- 1 Medium chopped onion
- 1 tsp Salt
- 1/2 tsp Allspice
- Beef casings

Preparation
- (Always served with an Irish "fry". The preparation of this pudding may be impractical these days due to the difficulty of procuring fresh pig's blood and casings.)
- Stew liver in boiling salted water until tender. Remove liver, and mince. Reserve cooking liquor. Mix all ingredients in large bowl. Stir thoroughly until blended.
- Fill casings with mixture. Tie off in one-foot loops. Steam for 4-5 hours. Leave until cold. Cut into 1/2 inch slices as required and fry in hot fat on both sides until crisped.

Boiled Collar of Bacon with Creamy Mustard Sauce

Ingredients
- 1 Kg unsmoked bacon
- 1 Medium onion
- 2 Carrots
- 2 Celery sticks
- Bay leaf
- 1 3/16 l Chicken stock
- 150 ml Double cream

- 70 gms Unsalted butter
- 1 tsp Brown mustard seeds
- Seasoning

Preparation
- Remove the rind from the bacon and roll the bacon. Roughly chop the onion, carrots and celery sticks. Make the chicken stock. Soak the bacon in water for 24 hours prior to cooking to reduce salt content Rinse well.
- Place the bacon in a pan with the vegetables and bay leaf. Cover with the stock or water. Bring to the simmer and continue simmering for 1-1.5 hours. Rest the bacon in the stock for 20-30 minutes.
- Drain off 600ml of stock and bring to the boil and reduce by half and serve with the bacon. Alternatively, add the cream, if using, to the reduced stock and cook for 10 minutes, then whisk in 25g of butter at a time, to taste.
- Add the mustard seeds, season and keep warm. Add the bacon, allowing 2 slices per person.

Bunratty

Ingredients
- 1 1/2 fl Irish whiskey
- 1 dash Sweet Martini
- 3/4 fl Irish Mist

Preparation
- Mix all ingredients over ice.

Cabbage and Bacon (Irish)

Ingredients
- 1 Lg (or 2 small Savoy cabbages)
- 8 Strips bacon
- 1 Salt and pepper
- 4 Whole allspice berries
- 300 ml Bacon (or chicken stock)

Preparation
- Cut the cabbage in half and boil for 15 minutes in salted water. Drain, and soak in cold water for 1minute, then drain well and slice.
- Line the bottom of a casserole with half the bacon strips, then put the

cabbage on top and add the seasonings.
- Add enough stock to barely cover, then put the remaining strips of bacon on top. Cover and simmer for an hour, until most of the liquid is absorbed.

Country Cork Irish stew

Ingredients
- 8 Small thawed lamb chops
- 1 Tsp vegetable oil
- 1Peppercorns thyme
- Rosemary
- 2 cups Finely Shredded cabbage
- 1 Sliced Large leek white thin
- 1 1/2 cup Diced celery stalks
- Chopped fresh parsley
- 1 Salt and pepper
- 1 Bay leaves Parsley
- 1 lb3 to 4 Medium potatoes
- 1 Medium chopped onion
- Small white onions
- 1 1/2 cup Peas

Preparation
- Season chops with salt and pepper. Heat oil in saucepan wide enough to hold all chops in a single layer. Brown on both sides. Spoon off any melted fat and add enough water to cover chops.
- Bring to a boil and add parsley, bay leaf, peppercorns, thyme and rosemary enclosed in cheesecloth. Lower heat and simmer. Meanwhile, peel potatoes and shape into bite sized rounds.
- Chop trimmings from potatoes into small pieces. Add potatoes, trimmings, cabbage, onion, well-rinsed leek, white onions and celery to chops and liquid. Simmer 20 minutes then add peas.
- Add a little more water if needed during cooking. Simmer 10 minutes more or until potatoes are tender. Correct seasoning. Garnish with parsley and serve.

Dijon-Glazed Corned Beef

Ingredients
- 2 1/2 lb Corned beef brisket
- 3 1/2 lb Same
- 2 tsp Dijon-style mustard

- 2 Tsp Honey
- 1 Tsp Orange juice concentrate
- Water

Preparation

- In Dutch oven, cover corned beef brisket with water. Cover Dutch oven tightly and simmer 2 1/2 to 3 1/2 hours or until tender. In cup, combine honey, defrosted orange juice concentrate and mustard and set aside.
- Remove brisket from cooking kiquid; trim fat from outer surface, if necessary. Position oven rack so that brisket on broiler pan rack is 3 to 4 inches from heat source.
- Brush glaze over brisket; broil 2 to 3 minutes or until glaze begins to caramelize. Carve brisket diagonally across the grain into thin slices.

Dressed Cabbage (Irish)

Ingredients

- 1 Cabbage
- 4 Tsp Butter
- 3 Tsp Bacon stock (or water)
- 1 pinch Nutmeg (or mace)
- 1/2 tsp Flour
- 1 Pepper

Preparation

- Shred the cabbage. Melt half the butter in a heavy pot; then add the cabbage and toss until covered with the butter.
- Add bacon stock or water, cover and cook gently for about 20 minutes. By this time the liquid should be nearly absorbed, and the cabbage cooked.
- Add the nutmeg or mace, the flour, and stir well; then add the rest of the butter and toss until melted into the cabbage. Add pepper if needed.

Dublin Sunday Corned Beef and Cabbage

Ingredients

- 5 lb Corned beef brisket
- 1 lg Onion stuck with 6 whole cloves
- 6 Peeled and sliced carrots
- 8 Peeled and cubed potatoes

- 1 tsp Dried thyme
- 1 Small bunch parsley
- Head Cabbage (about 2 lbs) cut in quarters
- Horseradish sauce
- 1/2 pt Whipping Cream
- Tsp to 3Tsp Prepared horseradish

Preparation

- Put beef in a large pot and cover with cold water. Add all other ingredients except cabbage and bring to a boil with the lid off the pot. Turn to simmer and cook for 3 hours.
- Skim fat from top as it rises. Remove the thyme, parsley and onion. Add cabbage. Simmer for 20 minutes until cabbage is cooked. Remove the meat and cut into pieces.
- Place on center of a large platter. Strain the cabbage and season it heavily with black pepper. Surround the beef with the cabbage, carrots and potatoes. Serve with horseradish sauce.
- Horseradish Sauce: Whip cream until it stands in peaks. Fold in horseradish.

Irish Beef in Guinness

Ingredients

- 2/3 lb Cubed beef
- 1/2 cup Flour seasoned with salt and pepper
- Oil for frying
- 2 Sliced onions
- 4 Minced cloves garlic
- 3 Sliced carrots
- 1 tsp Minced parsley
- 1/2 tsp Thyme
- To taste salt and pepper
- Beef broth (or stock)
- Bottles (12-oz each) Guinness

Preparation

- Dip beef in flour and coat on all sides. Brown in oil, in batches and remove to heat proof pot or casserole. Sauté onions and garlic in same oil and add to beef.
- Add carrots, parsley and thyme. Season with salt and pepper. Pour enough beef broth and Guiness to cover and bring to a boil. Reduce heat and simmer 30 minutes.

- Lift meat, onions and carrots from pot to serving plate with slotted spoon. Over high heat, reduce sauce to half the original volume. Pour sauce over meat and serve.

Irish Brogue

Ingredients
- 1 1/2 fl Irish whiskey
- 1/2 fl Bailey's Irish Cream

Preparation
- Fill a rocks glass with ice. Add ingredients and stir.

Irish Coffee No. 2

Ingredients
- 1 1/2 cup Warm water
- 1/4 cup Irish whiskey
- Dessert Topping
- 1 Tsp Instant coffee crystals
- 1 Brown Sugar to taste

Preparation
- Dessert topping should be in a pressurized can. In a 2-cup measure combine water and instant coffee crystals.
- Micro-cook, uncovered, on 100% power about 4 minutes or just till steaming hot. Stir in Irish whiskey and brown sugar. Serve in mugs. Top each mug of coffee mixture with some pressurized dessert topping.

Irish Handshake

Ingredients
- 1 fl Irish whiskey
- 1/2 fl Tia Maria
- 1/2 fl Green cream de menthe
- 1 Cream

Preparation
- Mix all ingredients except cream over ice and strain. Top with cream.

Irish Hot Pot

Ingredients
- 6 Medium Peeled thin Potatoes and sliced
- 2 Medium sliced onions thin
- 3 Sliced thin carrots scraped
- 1/4 cup Cooked rice not instant
- 1 can (14.5-oz) Peas with liquid
- 1 pkg. (20-oz) Sausage links/ground chuck in browned amounts you like
- 1 can (15-oz) Condensed cream of tomato soup diluted with a soup
- Water
- Salt
- White pepper to taste

Preparation
- In a buttered, 4 quart casserole layer the potatoes, onions and carrots, season each layer as you go with salt and pepper.
- Sprinkle with rice, then the peas with their liquid and top with the meat. Pour the diluted soup over all.
- Bake, covered, in a 375 degree oven for 1 hour. Remove cover, turn sausages and bake an additional hour, uncovered.

Irish Lamb Stew

Ingredients
- Boneless leg of lamb
- Medium chopped onions
- Tsp Flour
- 1 tsp Salt
- 1/4 tsp Rosemary
- 1 lb Cut into pieces potatoes
- 2 Small cubed rutabagas
- Jar of Boiled onions
- Tsp Oil
- Clove of minced garlic
- cups Beef stock

- Black pepper to taste
- 1 Bay leaf
- 6 Carrots sliced
- 1 lb Frozen peas

Preparation

- Cut lamb into cubes. Heat oil in a heavy saucepan, add lamb and cook until lightly browned, remove from pan. Add onion and garlic and cook for a few minutes. Add flour and stir, heat until mixture browns.
- Gradually add stock while stirring. Return meat to saucepan. Add salt, pepper, rosemary and bay leaf. Cover and simmer for 1 hour or until meat is almost tender. Add potatoes, carrots and turnips.
- Cook 30 minutes longer. Add peas and onions and continue cooking until peas are tender, about 10-15 minutes.

Simple Irish Stew

Ingredients

- 2 Tsp Oil
- 4 lg Onion cut in wedges
- 5 lg Carrots cut in thick slices
- 2 Rib sliced celery
- 1 1/2 lb Round steak (or lamb)
- 6 lg Potatoes
- 1 cup Water
- Salt and pepper to taste

Preparation

- Heat oil in large saucepan or skillet. Sauté onions in oil. Add carrots and celery and cook for a few minutes. Cut steak into 1/4 to 1/2 inch cubes and add to onions, carrots and celery.
- Wash, peel and slice potatoes and add to pot. Pour in water, season to taste with salt and pepper and bring to a boil. Skim of any foam, reduce heat and simmer over low heat until meat and vegetables are tender.
- NOTE: Can also cook in crock pot on low overnight, 7-8 hours, or on high for 3 4 hours. If desired, stew can be thickened by mixing 2 tablespoon flour with a little water and adding it to the stew. Heat through until thickened and serve piping hot.

Kidney Soup

Ingredients
- Beef kidney (about 1 1/2 lb)
- Tsp Bacon dripping (or oil)
- Tsp Flour
- 2 l Beef stock
- 1 Squeeze lemon juice
- 1 Spice bag
- Bouquet garni
- 1 Tsp Sugar
- Grind salt and pepper
- 1 Sliced Thinly carrot
- 1 Glass sherry

Preparation
- Spice bag should contain: 10 black peppercorns, 1 blade mace, pinch celery seed) should contain parsley, thyme and bay leaf.
- Skin the kidney, cut down the middle and remove the fatty core and any whitish membrane. (This is what can give a kidney a bad taste, so be thorough.)Heat the fat and brown the kidney in it quickly.
- Pour off any excess fat, and then stir in the flour, turning the kidney pieces in it. Cook for 1 minute, and then add the stock, sugar, bouquet garni, and the spice bag.
- Bring to the boil, then cover and simmer gently for about 3 hours. This can be done on the stove or in a crock pot. Cool the soup, then refrigerate.
- When it is quite cold take off any fat from the top, then remove the bouquet garni and spice bags. Taste for seasoning;   add the lemon juice and sherry if needed.
- If the pieces of kidney are not liked, strain the soup;   or it can be liquidized. Bring to just under boiling point before serving; serve with thin slices of dry toast, or cheese biscuits.

Oatmeal Bacon Pancakes

Ingredients
- 4 oz Flour
- oz Fine oatmeal
- 1 cup Buttermilk (or milk)
- 1 Egg (beaten)
- 8 Strips bacon

Preparation

- Sift the dry ingredients, and then add the egg and enough milk or buttermilk to make a batter like thick cream. Fry the bacon rashers and drain, then make a large pancake, pouring the batter over the entire bottom of the pan.
- Cook on one side, toss over, spread with a little mustard if liked, then add the bacon and fold over. Make the rest of the batter into pancakes the same way. Makes 4 very large pancakes or 8 small ones.

Savory Red Cabbage and Red Potatoes

Ingredients
- Small Head cabbage
- tsp Prepared horseradish
- 1 lb Small red potatoes
- 1/4 cup Butter
- Tsp Green onions/scallions
- 1/8 tsp Salt
- 1/8 tsp Pepper
- Water

Preparation
- In Dutch oven, place steamer basket over 1/2 inch deep water (water should not touch basket.) Cut cabbage (about 1 1/2 pounds) into 6 wedges and quarter potatoes.
- Place cabbage and potatoes in basket, cover tightly and heat water to boiling. Reduce heat to medium-low and steam 20-30 minutes or until tender.
- Meanwhile, in a 1 cup glass measure, combine butter, sliced green onions, horseradish, salt and pepper. Microwave on high 45 seconds or until butter is melted. Drizzle over vegetables.

Shamrock

Ingredients
- 3/4 fl Dry vermouth
- 1/2 fl Irish whiskey
- Green Chartreuse
- 3/4 fl Dry vermouth

- 1 dash Green cream de menthe

Preparation
- Mix all ingredients over i

Shannon Cream

Ingredients
- Bailey's Irish cream
- 1 dash Cream
- 1 dash Orange Curacao
- 1 Green cream de menthe

Preparation
- Mix ingredients over ice and top with cream de menthe.

Shannon Dove

Ingredients
- fl Irish whiskey
- 1 Cream
- Dash Tia Maria

Preparation
- Mix all ingredients except cream over ice and strain. Top with cream.

Steak and Guinness Pie

Ingredients
- 1 Kg Round steak
- 1 Tsp Flour
- 1 tsp Brown sugar
- 1 Tsp Raisins (optional)
- 5 Onions
- 300 ml Guinness
- 8 Slices bacon
- Lard chopped parsley

Preparation

- For double crust pie in deep pie dish. Cut the steak into bite sized cubes, roll in seasoned flour, and brown in the lard with the bacon, chopped small.
- Place the meat in a casserole, peel and chop the onions, and fry until golden before adding them to the meat.
- Add the raisins (if wanted) and brown sugar pour in the Guinness, cover tightly and simmer over a low heat or in a very moderate oven (325-350F) for 2 1/2 hours.
- Stir occasionally, and add a little more Guinness or water if the rich brown gravy gets too thick.
- Meanwhile, line a deep pie dish with half the pie crust: bake it blind: then add the Guinness/beef mixture from the casserole, cover with the top layer of pie crust, and bake until finished, and probably about 10 more minutes.
- Variation: for the brown sugar, substitute 3 T honey.

Trimlestown Roast Sirloin

Ingredients

- 3 lb Sirloin roast
- 2 fl Whiskey
- 10 fl Red wine
- oz Butter
- oz Flour
- 1 Salt and pepper

Preparation

- Preheat oven to 180C/350F. Wipe meat, season and place in a roasting pan. Place pan in oven and cook for one hour. Add the whiskey and wine to the pan.
- Cook for a further hour, basting once more. Remove the roast from the pan, place on a serving dish and keep warm. Pour off excess fat from the meat juices, adding water to bring to about 15 oz. beat the butter into the flour to form a smooth paste.
- Add a little of the juices to this and mix well, then pour onto juices, mixing again, and bring to the boil. Simmer gently for 2-3 minutes to cook flour. Correct the seasoning.
- If the sauce is too thick, add a little more water. Serve separately in a gravy boat. Jacket or mashed potatoes, and a cooked green vegetable (possibly broccoli) go well with this, since the sauce is so rich.

White Onion Soup

Ingredients
- 2 Tsp Butter
- lb Onions thinly sliced
- Cloves
- Tsp Flour (heaping)
- 1 pinch Powdered mace (or nutmeg)
- Bay leaf
- 1 l Chicken (or pork stock)
- 300 ml Milk
- 1 Salt and pepper
- 150 ml Cream
- Tsp Grated cheese (optional)

Preparation
- Heat the butter, and when foaming add the onions and cloves. Let the onions soften, but not color at all.
- Sprinkle over the flour, mix well and cook, stirring, for about 1 minute; then add the nutmeg, the bay leaf and the stock. Stir all the time until it boils, and see that it is smooth.
- Simmer until the onions are cooked, then gradually add the milk, stirring, and when that boils lift out the cloves and bay leaf.
- It can now be liquidized, or served as is with the cream added, and a sprinkling of grated cheese.

###

Part 9: Israeli Recipes

Israel's diverse population makes its cuisine unique. People from more than seventy different countries, with many different foods and customs, currently live in Israel. Many people began arriving in 1948, when the country, then known as Palestine, gained its independence from Great Britain. At that time, large numbers of Eastern European Jews hoped to establish a Jewish nation in Israel. They brought traditional Jewish dishes to Israel that had been prepared in countries like Poland, Hungary, and Russia. The Palestinians, most of whom were of Arab descent, enjoyed a cuisine adapted from North Africa and the Middle East

Halek
(Fruit and Nut Mix for Passover)

Ingredients
- 1/4 cup Almonds
- 1/4 cup Pistachio nuts
- 1/4 cup Walnuts
- 1/4 cup Pumpkin seeds
- 1/4 cup Hazelnuts
- 1/8 cup Coarsely chopped Pitted dates
- 1/8 cup Light and dark raisins
- 1/8 cup Coarsely chopped dried apricots
- 1/8 cup Chopped prunes
- 1/8 cup Aloo bukhara (dried apricots With seeds)
- 1/8 cup Coarsely chopped dried seeded cherries
- 1/4 cup Red wine
- 2 tsp Wine vinegar
- 1/4 tsp Advieh see recipe
- 1/4 tsp Rosewater

Preparation
- Coarsely chop the nuts in a processor. Mix the nuts, fruits, wine, vinegar, Advieh, and rosewater to achieve a moist, textured consistency.

Ghaime Bademjune
(Persian Chicken)

Ingredients
- 1 lb Chicken breasts
- 2 med Onions -- cut one in large pieces
- 1 Pie
- 1 For Cooking with chicken
- 1/2 cup Yellow split peas
- 6 oz Can tomato puree (or paste)
- 2 1/2 Dried lemons (you could
- 1 Dried substitute
- 3 1/2 Zucchini (or 1-2 eggplant) (Japanese preferred)

- 1 Thick (slice lengthwise)
- Salt
- Oil

Preparation
- Fry onion. Cook chicken in water with onion. When well done add fried onion and split peas. After cooked well, add tomato paste/puree, dried lemon peel, and simmer till very well done.
- Fry zucchini and eggplant slices in oil with turmeric after sprinkling with salt. Put chicken and sauce in dish and place veggie slices on top. Warm in oven or microwave. Serve with Hot basmati rice.

Haroseth Para Pesach
(Passover Haroseth)

Ingredients
- 3/4 cup Raisins
- 2 lb Seeded dates
- 1 Peeled and sliced apple
- 1 cup Not too dry red wine

Preparation
- Grind the fruit together. Add the wine and mix well. Place on the Seder table. The Ashkenazi Jews of Europe use the word "Haroseth" for this Passover ritual dish. The Indians and Persians call it "halek".

Israeli Burekas
(Pronounced Buh-Ray-Kahs)

Ingredients
- 1 1 pkg. Prepared strudel dough
- 1 Or puff pastry
- 1 Sesame seeds (optional)
- 1 Cheese filling
- 1 cup Grated cheddar cheese
- 1 cup Grated white salty cheese
- 1 (Feta (or salty goat)
- 1 Cheese)
- 1 Egg

- 1 Egg yolk and Beaten
- 1 Tsp Water (to brush on top)

Preparation
- Mix together the cheese and egg. Set aside. Divide pastry dough in half. Roll out and stretch to form a large rectangle. Cut into 4-inch squares.
- Place a heaping spoonful of cheese mixture in the center of each square. Fold over to form a triangle. Pinch edges together firmly; brush tops of each with egg yolk mix and sprinkle with sesame seeds, if desired.
- Bake on lightly greased cookie sheet at 350 degrees for about 30 minutes, or until golden brown. Makes about 20 burekas. Serve hot.
- These are delicious for breakfast or lunch. Made smaller they serve as tasty appetizers. I have given the recipe for cheese burekas here, but a great many other fillings are equally good.
- Be creative. To mashed potatoes add a dash of onion powder and some parsley flakes. Many people love spinach fillings or sautéed mushrooms.
- My own family likes a sweet cheese filling made with egg and sugar (to taste), added to cream cheese.

Kebseh

Ingredients
- 3 Tsp olive oil
- 1 lg Chopped onion
- 1 Minced clove garlic
- 3 Pods cardamom
- 1 Cinnamon stick
- 1/4 tsp Ground cumin
- 1 1/2 lb Cubed lamb
- 1 Salt
- 1 lb Ripe tomatoes
- 1 cup Water
- 1/4 cup Low-fat yoghurt
- 1 Serrano pepper (optional)
- 1 cup Soaked uncooked rice
- 1 Pepper

Preparation
- Sauté the onion in the olive oil until soft and transparent. Stir the spices into the oil to release the flavors. Cook for a minute or two.
- Raise the heat and add the lamb, sprinkling with salt. Sauté until browned

on all sides. Whirl the fresh tomatoes in a food processor or blender until nearly smooth, and add to the meat.

- Stir in the water, yoghurt, garlic and serrano pepper. Taste and adjust the seasoning. Cover and simmer about 2 hours until the meat is tender.
- The tomato sauce will reduce somewhat. After cooking 2 hours, measure the liquid. The amount of rice that needs to be added is based on the amount of liquid.
- Example: If sauce has 2 cups of liquid; then add 1 cup of rice. Can add more water if needed. Add rice and bring back to a boil.
- Cover saucepan with a dish towel (to absorb moisture) and replace lid. Simmer for approximately 20 minutes until moisture is gone and rice is done. Do not stir during this 20 minute process!

Kibbe
(Baked)

Ingredients
- 2 lb Cut into large boneless leg of lamb (no fat or gristle)
- 2 cups Fine bulgur wheat
- 4 cups Water
- 2 lg Peeled yellow onions
- 2 Tsp Chopped parsley
- 1/2 tsp Salt
- 1/4 tsp Ground allspice
- 1/4 tsp Ground cinnamon
- 2 Tsp Fresh mint (or 1 tsp)-Chopped
- 1/4 cup Chilled water
- 1 Stuffing
- 1/2 lb Boneless leg of lamb (no fat or gristle)
- 2 Tsp Butter
- 1/4 cup Pine nuts
- 1 med Chopped peeled and finely yellow onion
- 1/8 tsp Ground cinnamon
- 1/8 tsp Ground allspice
- 1 Freshly Ground salt and
- 1 To Taste black pepper
- 5 Tsp Olive oil

Preparation
- Soak the bulgur in 4 cups water for 1/2 hour. Drain well. Prepare kibbe mixture as above. Stuffing: Grind the lamb coarsely in your meat grinder.

- Sauté the lamb in the butter into the moisture has evaporated, then add all the other ingredients except the oil and continue cooking until the onions are transparent.
- Oil a 9x13-inch glass baking dish well with 2 tbsp of the olive oil. Spread a 1/4 inch layer of the raw kibbe evenly in the bottom.
- Keep your hands moist and the kibbe will spread more evenly and smoothly. Next, spread all the stuffing evenly over the bottom layer.
- Form the remaining raw kibbe into 1-inch-thick patties and lay them over the stuffing. With your hands still moist, join the patties and smooth them into a layer (thick) to cover the stuffing.
- Using a paring knife, score lines about 1/4 inch deep into the meat, making 1-inch-long diamond patterns all over. Lightly cover with the remaining 3 tbsp of olive oil.
- Bake in a preheated 400 F oven for 20 minutes. Reduce heat to 300 F and bake for at least 30 minutes, or until golden brown. To serve, cut the meat into 3 pieces.

###

Part 10: Middle Eastern Recipes

The Middle East was where wheat was first cultivated, followed by barley, pistachios, figs, pomegranates, dates and other regional staples. Fermentation was also discovered to leaven bread and make beer. As a crossroads between Europe, Asia and Africa, the Middle East has long been a hub of food and recipe exchange. During the Persian Empire (ca. 550–330 BCE) the foundation was laid for Middle Eastern food when rice, poultry, and fruits were incorporated into their *diets.*

Lebanese Cabbage Rolls

Ingredients
- 1 Serving
- 1 lg Head cabbage
- 1 lb Coarsely ground beef
- 1 cup Rice
- 2 tsp Salt
- 1 Juice of 2 lemons
- 1/4 tsp m.s.g.
- 1/2 tsp Allspice
- 3 Cloves garlic
- 2 cup Canned tomatoes (or 1 can)
- 1 Tomato
- 1 Paste

Preparation
- Preparation: Wash rice and drain. Add meat and 1 cup tomatoes or ½ can paste. Add salt, pepper and spices.
- This is the filling. Separate cabbage leaves and drop separately in salted boiling water and cook a few minutes until limp.
- Cook all leaves then let drain. Trim leaves of heavy stems. Reserve stems and put in bottom of saucepan.
- On each leaf place 1 heaping tbsp. of filling and roll firmly. Place cabbage rolls neatly in rows making several layers.
- Place garlic buds among leaves as you roll. Add 1 cup tomatoes and enough hot water to cover rolls.
- Sprinkle 1/2 tsp. salt over all. Cook 45 minutes to 1 hour. During last 15 minutes of cooking, add the juice

Abgushte Miveh
(Dried Fruit Soups)

Ingredients
- 1 lb Lamb (or beef stew meat) -Lean

- 1 lb Lamb (or beef soup bones)
- 7 cups Water
- 1 Limu omani (dried lime) -optional
- 1 Freshly ground black pepper
- 2 Tsp Ghee (or butter)
- 1 lg Finely chopped onion
- 2 tsp Turmeric
- 1 cup Pitted prunes
- 1/2 cup Dried apricot halves
- 1/2 cup Chopped dried peaches
- 1/3 to 1/2 cup Brown sugar
- 1 to 2 tsp Lemon (or lime -juice)

Preparation

- Cut meat into small cubes and place in a soup pot with bones, water, and dried lime if available. Bring slowly to the boil, skimming when necessary.
- Add salt and pepper, cover and simmer gently for 1 1/2 hours or until meat is almost tender. Remove bones and dried lime if used.
- In a frying pan, heat ghee or butter and fry onion until transparent, stir in turmeric, and cook until lightly browned.
- Add to soup with dried fruits (these may be washed if necessary, but do not require soaking). Cover and simmer for 30 minutes.
- Add sugar and lemon or lime juice to taste so that soup has a pleasant sweet-sour flavor. Serve hot.

Almond Falafel

Ingredients

- 1 1/2 lb Ground lean lamb
- 1 sm Diced eggplant (3/4 lb.)
- 1 Chopped tomato -- coarsely
- 1 1/2 tsp Salt
- 1 cup Yogurt
- 1/4 cup Grated parmesan cheese
- 1 lg Onion
- 1 Minced clove garlic
- 2 Tsp Dry red wine
- 1/2 tsp Cinnamon
- 1 cup Chopped almonds -- toasted
- 3 (8 inch)
- 1 Halved pita breads

Preparation

- In Dutch oven brown lamb with onion, eggplant and garlic over medium heat about 5 minutes. Drain off excess fat.
- Stir in tomato, wine, salt and cinnamon. Continue to cook, covered, for about 20 minutes until vegetables are tender, stirring occasionally.
- Stir in yogurt, almonds, and cheese. Spoon 1 cup hot lamb mixture in each 1/2 of pita bread. Serve immediately.

Arkayagan Abour
(Meatball Soup)

Ingredients

- 6 Servings
- 1/2 lb Lean venison (or lamb)
- 1 Ground twice
- 1/2 cup Ground wheat cooked rice
- 1 Or bulghour
- 1/4 cup Chopped finely onion
- 1/4 cup Chopped finely parsley
- 2 cans Condensed chicken broth
- 1 (10-1/2 Ounces each)
- 2 cans Water
- 1/3 cup Lemon juice
- 2 Eggs
- 1 Pepper salt

Preparation

- Combine first four ingredients. Shape into 3/4-inch balls. Heat broth and water to the simmering point. Add meatballs; simmer 15 to 20 minutes.
- In a soup tureen, beat lemon juice and eggs until smooth. Gradually beat in hot broth. Add meatballs last. Season to taste with salt, pepper.

Ash Sak
(Lamb & Spinach Soup with Meatballs)

Ingredients

- 3 lb Sawed meat lamb bones
- 6 cups Water
- 1/2 lb Finely chopped fresh, washed, trimmed spinach

- 1 Defrosted or 10 oz. pkg chopped frozen spinach
- 2 cups finely chopped and preferably flat leaf parsley
- 1 cup coarsely chopped onion
- 1/2 cup Drained Iranian rice or other long grain rice, raw, soaked
- 1 Tsp Finely fresh cut or 1 teaspoon dried dill weed dill
- 4 tsp Salt
- 1 Freshly ground black pepper
- 1/2 cup Dried yellow split peas
- 1/2 tsp Turmeric
- Meatballs:
- 1/2 lb Lean ground lamb
- 2 tbs Iranian rice long grain rice or raw
- 2 tbs Finely chopped parsley
- 1 tbs Dried yellow split peas
- 1 tsp Finely chopped onion
- 1/4 tsp Turmeric
- 1/2 tsp Salt
- 1 Egg garnish:
- 1/2 cup Olive oil
- 2 med Peeled and cut into onion
- 1/4 Inch thick slices
- 6 tbs Butter
- 4 tbs Finely fresh cut mint or 2 tablespoons dried mint
- 2 tsp Turmeric
- 2 cups Unflavored at room temperature yoghurt

Preparation

- Soup: In a heavy 8 to 10 quart casserole, combine the lamb bones and water and bring to a boil over high heat, meanwhile skimming off the foam and scum as they rise to the surface.
- Then stir in the spinach, the 2 cups of parsley, 1 cup of onions, 1/2 cup of rice, dill, 4 teaspoon turmeric, cover tightly and simmer for 1 hour longer.
- (Check the casserole form time to time and add more water if necessary; the ingredients should be well covered with liquid throughout the cooking period.)
- Meatballs: Combine the ground lamb, 2 tablespoons of rice, 2 tablespoons of parsley, 1 tablespoon split peas, 1 teaspoon onion, 1/4 teaspoon turmeric, 1/2 teaspoon salt and the egg in a deep bowl.
- Knead vigorously with both hands, then beat with a wooden spoon until fairly smooth. Moistening your hands in cold water occasionally, shape the mixture into balls about 1 inch in diameter.
- (There will be about 24 meatballs.) When the soup has cooked for 2 hours, gently drop in the meatballs and simmer tightly covered for about 30 minutes.

- Garnish: About 15 minutes before the meatballs are done, heat 1/2 cup of olive oil in a heavy 10 to 12 inch skillet until a light haze forms above it.
- Add the sliced onions and, stirring frequently, cook over moderate heat for about 10 minutes, or until the onions are deeply browned. Set aside.
- In a small skillet or saucepan, melt the butter over low heat without letting it brown. Remove the pan from the heat and stir in the mint and 2 teaspoons of turmeric.
- For each serving, spoon about 1/4 cup of the yoghurt into a heated soup plate and ladle 2 cups of soup over it.
- Add 1 tablespoon of the melted butter and mint mixture, and stir until all the ingredients are well combined.
- Arrange 3 of the meatballs in each serving or the soup and sprinkle the top with a few of the browned onions. Serve at once.

Ash-E Jow
(Iranian Barley Soup)

Ingredients
- 1 cup Dried barley
- 1/2 cup Dried green (or red lentils)
- 6 cups Water
- 2 med Diced onions
- 2 Tsp Olive (or sunflower oil)
- 1 Tsp Dried mint (or parsley)
- 1 tsp Turmeric
- 1/2 tsp Ground black pepper

Preparation
- Put everything into a pot and then bring to a gentle boil. Simmer for 1 1/4 hours, stirring occasionally. Serve with feta cheese and salad.
- Variations: Fry the onions, in the oil, before putting them in the pot. Add 1 cup of cooked chick peas or red kidney beans, a few minutes before serving.

Turkish Spicy Eggs

Ingredients
- 2 Finely sliced onions
- 1 Cored &yellow pepper

- 1 Sliced
- 2 Cored & sliced red peppers
- 2 Chopped cloves garlic
- 2 Chopped chilies
- 1/2 tsp Cumin seeds
- 3 Tsp Oil
- 4 Eggs
- 1 Salt & pepper
- 1 Greek yoghurt

Preparation

- Fry the vegetables and spices in olive oil until the peppers are soft and juicy. Season with salt.
- One at a time break the eggs into a saucer and then slip into the nest of peppers.
- Cook until the whites of the egg are set. Serve from the pan with a dollop of yoghurt.

Baked Kibbeh

Ingredients

- 1/2 cup Bulgar wheat
- 2 cups Hot water
- 1/4 cup Finely chopped onion
- 3/4 tsp Salt
- 1/2 tsp Ground cinnamon
- 1/4 to 1/2 tsp. Ground pepper
- 1 1/2 lb Ground ground lamb (or beef)
- 3/4 cup Finely chopped onion
- 1/3 cup Pine nuts (or almonds) -slivered
- 1 tsp Lemon juice
- 1/2 to 1 tsp. Salt
- 1 dash Pepper
- 1 Plain yogurt

Preparation

- Soak bulgar (wheat) in water for 1 hour. Drain well; squeeze out excess water. Stir in the 1/4 cup chopped onion, the 3/4 teaspoon salt, cinnamon, and 1/4 to 1/4 teaspoon pepper.
- Add 1 pound of the ground meat; mix well. Set aside. In a skillet cook remaining meat, the 3/4 cup chopped onion, and nuts till meat is brown.
- Drain off fat. Stir in lemon juice, the 1/2 to 1 teaspoon salt, and the dash

pepper. In a 10x6x2-inch baking dish press half of the meat-bulgar mixture evenly over the bottom.
- Top with cooked meat-nut mixture. Cover with remaining meat-bulgur mixture, pressing down with hands.
- Bake in 350 degree F. oven about 25 minutes or till done. Drain off fat. Serve warm or chilled with yogurt. Makes 6 servings.

Beet Relish (Turkey)
(Kuchundooria)

Ingredients
- 1 Beets
- 1 Boiling water
- 1 med Quartered and sliced onion
- 1 Cider vinegar
- 1 tsp Salt

Preparation
- Beets prepared this way are used as a relish with meat. Wash beets thoroughly. Top the beets, leaving 1 inch of the stems to retain color.
- Retain some of the stems that were cut off. Cover the beets with boiling water and cook till tender. Young beets will cook in 30-60 minutes, depending on size.
- Place the cooked beets in a pan of cold water and slip off their skins. Cut the beets in quarters and put them in a bowl or jar with one medium onion.
- Add cider vinegar blended with double the amount of boiled water to cover and 1 teaspoon of salt. Serve cold as a relish with chicken or meat.

Bulgur Meatballs
(Keftede)

Ingredients
- 3/4 cup Bulgur
- 1/2 cup Cooked chickpeas -- 4 oz
- 1 lb Ground lamb -- lean
- 1/2 cup bread crumbs
- 1 (Crumbled bread finely pita)
- 1 lg Beaten egg -- slightly
- 1/4 cup Fresh lemon juice
- 1 Crushed clove garlic

- 1 1/2 tsp Ground coriander
- 1 tsp Ground cumin
- 1/2 tsp Salt
- 1/4 tsp White pepper
- 1/4 cup Chopped parsley -- (or mint)
- 1 Or mix
- 3 Tsp Virgin olive oil – (or less)
- 1 Sprig fresh mint -- for garnish
- 1 For garnish salad leaves
- 1/3 cup Plain low fat yogurt

Preparation

- PREPARATION (30 minutes) - Place the bulgur in a small bowl, add enough cold water to cover and let soak for 10 minutes.
- Drain through a sieve lined with a piece of cheesecloth. Wrap the cheesecloth around the bulgur and squeeze out the excess water.
- OR USE INSTANT Place the chickpeas in a blender or a food processor fitted with a metal blade and blend until finely chopped. (Or coarse chop)
- COOKING (30 minutes chilling and 30 minutes cooking) Place the bulgur, chickpeas, lamb, bread crumbs, egg, lemon juice, garlic, coriander, cumin, salt, pepper and mint in a large mixing bowl and combine well.
- With cold, wet hands, roll the mixture into 30 balls, about 1-1/2 in (3 cm) in diameter. Place on a large plate, cover and refrigerate for at least 20 minutes.
- Re-roll the chilled meatballs, if necessary, to refine the shape. Heat half the oil in a large, non-stick skillet over medium heat.
- Reduce the heat to low, add half the meatballs and cook, moving and turning over frequently, until browned on all sides and cooked in the center, about 6 to 8 minutes.
- Test one for pink-center. Transfer to paper toweling when done. Cover with foil to keep warm. - Heat the remaining oil in the skillet and cook the remaining meatballs.
- Place meatballs on a warm serving platter. Serve hot, garnished with mint and salad leaves or dandelion greens. Serve with yogurt in a bowl.

Casserole of Veal (Turkey)
(Dana Tas Etli Kebabi)

Ingredients
- 2 lb Sliced boned leg of veal
- 2 Tsp Chopped onion

- 1 tsp Salt
- 1/2 tsp Pepper
- 2 Tsp Fresh coconut or canned
- 1 Flaked coconut
- 1/4 tsp Thyme
- 1/4 tsp Ground cloves
- 1/4 cup Chicken fat (or olive oil)
- 2 Peeled tomatoes
- 1 cup Dry white wine

Preparation
- Wipe off the meat and cut into thick chunks, about 2 inches square. Place in a shallow casserole or skillet with the onion, salt, pepper, coconut, thyme and cloves.
- Mix thoroughly and put aside in a cool place for 2 hours. Heat the fat or olive oil and add it to the meat in the casserole. Sauté for 3 minutes, moving the pan continuously.
- Add the tomatoes and wine. Cover tightly. Cook over low heat 3-4 hours till meat is tender. Serve hot with white or saffron rice. Serves

Hummus
(With Sun-Dried Tomatoes and Cilantro)

Ingredients
- 1 cup Chick-peas
- 3 lg Chopped garlic cloves
- 1/4 cup Lemon juice
- 3 Tsp Olive oil or
- 2 Tsp Olive oil and
- 1 Tsp Chili flavored olive oil
- 3 Tsp Sesame tahini
- 1/4 cup Plain low-fat yogurt
- 1/2 cup Cumin
- 4 Sun-dried tomatoes in oil
- 1 Chopped roughly
- 1/4 cup Finely fresh cilantro
- 1 Chopped
- 1 Salt
- 1 ds Cayenne pepper
- 1 Chopped some finely fresh

- 1 Cilantro

Preparation
- 2 1/2 cups cooked chick-peas (1 cup dried), drained (reserve some of the liquid) or 15-ounce can, drained (reserve some of the liquid)
- Chop the garlic in a food processor fitted with the steel blade. Add the chick-peas. Process for about a minute, until the chick-peas are chopped and mealy.
- Add the lemon juice, olive oil, tahini, half of the yogurt and a dash of cayenne pepper. Process until smooth. Thin out as desired with the remaining yogurt and some extra olive oil.
- The mixture should be smooth but not runny. If the mixture seems too dry, add a bit of the reserved liquid from the chick-peas or a bit more oil.
- Remove mixture from the food processor and place in bowl. Stir in the chopped sun-dried tomatoes and the finely chopped cilantro. Taste and adjust seasonings.
- Garnish with the extra chopped cilantro. Serve with raw vegetables and/or pita bread sliced into triangular wedges.
- Water

Preparation
- Fry lentils in 2 tbsp. oil for about 2 minutes, stirring constantly. Add 3 c. water, salt, pepper and garlic powder. Cover and let simmer for about 40 minutes.
- Meanwhile, in another pan, fry rice in 2 tbsp. oil. Add 2 1/2 c. water and 2 tsp. chicken bouillon. Cover and simmer slowly about 20 minutes.
- When both rice and lentils are done, mix together and add more seasoning if necessary.
- For an added treat, fry another onion in a little oil or margarine and sprinkle over the top of lentils/rice just before serving.

Lebanese Baba Ghanoush

Ingredients
- 1 lg About 1 unpeeled eggplant
- 1 lb
- 1 lg Peeled and clove garlic
- 1 Crushed
- 2 Tsp Tahini (sesame paste)
- 1 Juice of 1/2 lemon (or to)
- 1 Taste
- 1 To taste salt

- 1 Garnishes
- 3 Tsp Olive oil
- 1 Cut into wedges pita bread
- 1 Chopped parsley

Preparation

- Using a fork, poke the eggplant at least a dozen times. Place on a baking sheet and broil on all sides about 4 to 5 inches from the source of heat.
- Turn often until the eggplant is browned nicely all over. Total time will be about 45 minutes. Remove the eggplant from the broiler and allow to cool for a few minutes.
- Cut the eggplant in half lengthwise, and scoop out the soft insides, discarding the browned peel.
- In a bowl mash the eggplant and the remaining ingredients, except the garnishes, with a fork. Do not use a food processor or blender as you do not want too smooth a paste.
- Serve on a plate with the olive oil and parsley sprinkled over the top. Guests dip the bread wedges into the Baba Ghanoush and go directly to heaven without passing go! Serves 4-6 as an appetizer.

Falafel

Ingredients

- 1 cup dried chickpeas or 16 oz. can of chickpeas or garbanzo beans.
- 1 large Chopped onion
- 2 Chopped cloves of garlic
- 3 Chopped tablespoons of fresh parsley
- 1 teaspoon Coriander
- 1 teaspoon Cumin
- 2 tablespoons Flour Salt Pepper Oil for frying

Preparation

- Place dried chickpeas in a bowl, covering with cold water. Allow to soak overnight. Omit this step if using canned beans. Drain chickpeas, and place in pan with fresh water, and bring to a boil.
- Allow to boil for 5 minutes, then let simmer on low for about an hour. Drain and allow to cool for 15 minutes. Combine chickpeas, garlic, onion, coriander, cumin, salt and pepper (to taste) in medium bowl.
- Add flour. Mash chickpeas, ensuring to mix ingredients together. You can also combine ingredients in a food processor. You want the result to be a thick paste.
- Form the mixture into small balls, about the size of a ping pong ball.

Slightly flatten. Fry in 2 inches of oil at 350 degrees until golden brown (5-7 minutes).

-
- Serve hot. Serving Suggestion Falafel can be served as an appetizer with hummus and tahini, or as a main course.
- Stuff pita bread with falafel, lettuce, tomatoes, tahini, salt and pepper. As an alternative, falafel can be formed into patties and served like a burger. Serves 4.

Ghormeh Sabzi
(Vegetable Stew)

Ingredients
- 1 bunch Fresh spinach (esfenag)
- 1/2 bunch Fresh dill (sheveed)
- 1 bunch Fresh parsely (ja`faree)
- 1 bunch Fresh cilantro (or coriantro)
- 1 (Geshneez)
- 1 bunch (Use only the green stems)
- 1 Fresh leak (tareh farangee)
- 1 bunch Fresh chives (tareh)
- 1 bunch Scallions (piazcheh).
- 1 Dried table spoon
- 1 Shanbelileh
- 1 lb Cubed stew meat (beef, lamb, veal, etc).
- 4 Dried or tablespoon lemon dried lemons (limoo amanee)
- 1 med finely chopped. onion
- 1/2 tsp Turmeric (zard choobeh).
- 3 Tsp cooking oil.
- 1 Tsp Lemon juice (optional).
- 1 cup Beans pre-soaked or Dried can
- 1 Pepper touch each of salt
- 1 and red peppers

Preparation
- Wash and cube the meat and let it drain. Cut off the heads of the leaks (and scallions) and put the stems along with the rest of vegetables in a kitchen stringer, thoroughly was and let them drain.
- Using a cutting board, while repeatedly bunching up all vegetables together, finely chop the vegetables. The smaller the pieces the better.
- Place the chopped vegetables in a pot, put the heat setting to high, and frequently stir the vegetables until all their excess water has evaporated.

- Add two table spoons of cooking oil and continually stir fry the vegetables until they turn a reddish color. This process should take about 15 minutes.
- Take the pot off the heat and put it aside. During the stir fry process, you may add a bit more oil if needed. When finished, the vegetables resemble dried ones with no water remaining in the pot.
- In another pot, add about one table spoon of cooking oil and the chopped onions and stir fry over medium heat, until they turn a golden brown color.
- Add the meat, stir fry for a few minutes, add salt, pepper and turmeric and let the meat fry with the onions for a few minutes.
- If you are using dried beans, at this point drain them and add them to the mixture. Next poke a hole in each of the dried lemons and add them to the mixture (or add the powdered kind).
- Add about two cups (16 oz) of water, place the lid on the pot and let it boil for another 15 minutes. Add the fried vegetables into the mixture, turn the heat setting to medium-low and let it cook.
- The cooking time required from this point on is about another hour. Half way through this period, if you are using canned beans, add them into the mixture.
- Once the meat is separated when poked by a fork, the stew is ready. This stew is served over white rice.

Baked Guavas
(Stuffed With Mushrooms & Olives)

Ingredients
- 6 Guavas
- 1 Tsp Oil
- 1 cup Chopped mushrooms
- 1 Tsp Chopped onion
- 1/2 cup Chopped green olives
- 2 Tsp Chopped parsley
- 4 tsp Fresh dill weed or Chopped
- 1 tsp Dried dill
- 1/2 tsp Each salt and pepper
- 1 Tsp Sesame seeds

Preparation
- To prepare the guavas for stuffing, cut a thin slice from the top of the guava. With a melon ball scoop or small spoon, remove the seeds and set the guavas aside.
- Heat the oil in a skillet. Add mushrooms, onion, green olives, herbs, salt and pepper; sauté until vegetables are soft. Remove the mixture from the

flame; cool.
- Stuff the guavas, filling them to the top. Place stuffed guavas in a baking dish just large enough to hold them and sprinkle sesame seeds over the guava tops. Bake at 325 F. for 1 hour, or until the fruit is tender. Serve hot.

Lebanese Yogurt and Cucumber Salad

Ingredients
- 3 cups Plain yogurt
- 12 Fresh mint leaves
- 2 Peeled cloves garlic
- 1 To Taste salt
- 3 Peeled and thinly cucumbers
- 1 Sliced

Preparation
- Drain the yogurt in a cheesecloth-lined colander for several hours, discarding the liquid that has collected.
- Place the mint and garlic together in a salad bowl and crush with a little salt. Add the drained yogurt and cucumbers. Mix and chill before serving. Serves 6-8 as a salad or dip.

Yemenite Meat Loaf (Halabi Kebab)

Ingredients
- 2 1/2 lb Ground beef
- 3 Tsp Flour
- 1 Tsp Oil
- 1 tsp Salt
- 1 tsp Pepper
- 1 Tsp Zhoug
- 3 Tsp Oil
- 1 cup Chopped finely onions
- 1 cup Sliced mushrooms
- 1 cup Chopped parsley
- 3 Eggs

Preparation
- Combine ground beef with flour, 1 tbsp oil, salt, pepper and zhoug. Form the meat mixture into a 10-inch loaf.
- Make a well the entire length of the loaf. Heat 3 tbsp of oil in a skillet.

- Sauté together the onions, mushrooms and parsley until the onions are golden.
- Place the mixture in the well of the loaf. Lightly beat the eggs and pour over the vegetables. Preheat oven to 350 degrees.
- Pat the sides of the loaf together to close up the well, and wrap in aluminum foil. Bake for 30 minutes. The loaf may be served hot or cold.

Turkish Mussels
(With Garlic & Walnut Sauce)

Ingredients
- 2 lb Mussels
- 1 Seasoned flour
- 2 lightly beaten eggs
- 1 Sun flower oil for frying
- 1 Sauce
- 2 slices crust stale white bread
- 1 Remove
- 3 Crushed cloves garlic
- 2 Tsp White wine vinegar
- 2 oz Finely ground walnuts
- 6 Tsp Olive oil
- 1 Salt

Preparation
- Make sauce. Soak the bread in water for 10 minutes. Drain and gently squeeze out the water.
- In a liquidiser whizz the bread with the garlic, vinegar, nuts and salt until smooth. Gradually drizzle in the olive oil.
- Taste and adjust the seasoning. Clean the mussels well and rinse thoroughly. Heat 1/2 " water in a large wide pan until boiling.
- Add the mussels, cover tightly and shake over a high heat for a few minutes until they have opened. Remove mussels from shell and reserve.
- Carefully thread the mussels onto wooden skewers that have been presoaked in water for 30 minutes.
- Put on about 6 mussels per skewer and don't pack too tightly. Coat each skewerful first in seasoned flour, then in beaten egg and finally in flour again.
- Make sure that it is coated thoroughly each time. Fry in hot oil, turning occasionally with tongs, until golden brown. Drain briefly on kitchen paper and serve immediately with the sauce.

Turkish Menemen

Ingredients
- 2 Small tomatoes
- 1 Small bell pepper
- 1 Spicy pepper
- 1 Onion (optional)
- 4 - 5 Pitted and diced olives (optional
- 1 tbsp Olive oil
- 4 - 5 Eggs

Preparation
- Peel and cube tomatoes. Then cube other ingredients (fine) and sauté in small pre-heated skillet with olive oil.
- Until slightly wilted (don't totally kill the crunch!)then over low heat crack eggs into the skillet and scramble in the skillet cooking until eggs are fairly firm but the entire dish is slightly moist due to the vegetable juices.
- This is probably the most popular egg dish in Turkey and certainly the most popular one that can be made without uniquely
- Turkish ingredients that could be hard to find. Try it, and I think you'll like it, but it's guaranteed to taste better.
- Mediterranean or the Bosphorus over your shoulder, so come to Turkey for the original

Turkish Imam Biayeldi

Ingredients
- 3 med aborigines (1 1/2 lb)
- 1 lb Thinly sliced onions
- 5 Chopped garlic cloves
- 1 Finely
- 1 Sunflower oil
- 1 Thinly sliced green pepper
- 1 (optional)
- 1 Good quality tomato juice
- 8 oz Peeled and tomatoes
- 1 Chopped
- 1 Pepper
- 1 tsp Sugar
- 1 lg Chopped bunch parsley
- 1 lg Sliced tomato

Preparation

- Cut aubergines in half lengthways. Sprinkle with salt and leave for 30 mins. Rinse and pat dry. Preheat oven to 200 C (gas 6).
- To make stuffing gently fry onions and garlic in 3 tbsps oil until soft. Add the green pepper and tomatoes, seasoned with salt, pepper, and a little sugar.
- Cook gently for about 15 mins and stir in the parsley. Quickly shallow fry the aubergines in hot oil enough to seal them, turning to brown all over.
- Drain on kitchen paper. Make a deep slit along the length of the aubergine halves. Open the slit and spoon in as much stuffing as the slit will hold.
- Lay the aubergine halves close to each other in a baking dish and garnish with tomato slices.
- Pour in enough tomato juice to almost cover the aubergines and bake for about 45 mins. Serve at room temperature

Tabouli
(Bulgur Wheat Salad)

Ingredients

- 1 cup Whole wheat bulgur
- 1 lg Chopped onion
- 1 Boiling water
- 1 lb chopped or 1*16*oz tomatoes
- 1 can Diced tomatoes
- 1/2 cup Lemon juice
- 1/4 tsp Black pepper
- 1 Salt

Preparation

- Put 1 cup of whole wheat bulgur and 1 large chopped onion in a medium Pyrex bowl and cover with boiling water...let these soak 2 hours
- Drain well and add 1 lb of fresh chopped tomatoes or one 16 oz can of diced tomatoes, 1/3 cup lemon juice (freshly squeezed tastes much better than from concentrate)
- 1/4 tsp or more freshly ground black pepper, and salt to taste. Let it stand for several hours or overnight in the refrigerator to mix the flavors.

Syrian Wheat Pudding

Ingredients
- 1 1/2 cups Bugler (cracked wheat)
- 4 cups Water
- 1 cup Raisins
- 1/2 tsp Caraway seeds
- 1 Tsp Shelled pistachio nuts
- 1 Tsp Shelled chopped walnuts
- 1/4 cup Maple syrup

Preparation
- Place bulgar, water, raisins, and caraway seeds in a covered pot. Cook over medium heat for 30 minutes.
- Stir occasionally. Add nuts and syrup. Simmer 5 minutes longer. Serve warm.

Syrian Sausage in Pita

Ingredients
- 2 lb Ground once leg of lamb
- 2 Tsp Chopped fresh tarragon
- 2 tsp Ground coriander seed
- 1 tsp Allspice
- 2 Tsp Red wine
- 1/4 cup Pine nuts
- 1 Tsp Salt
- 1/2 tsp Pepper
- 1 Feet narrow sausage casing
- 1 Butter and olive oil
- 6 Individual pita rounds
- 1 Chopped bunch coriander

Preparation
- To make the sausage meat, combine the first eight ingredients in a large bowl. Mix well with your hands.
- Using a sausage stuffer or a pastry bag, stuff the casings, twisting every 3 inches. Saute the sausage in a mixture of half butter and half olive oil until brown, turning occasionally.
- Serve in pita rounds, sprinkled with plenty of chopped coriander. Makes 6 servings.

Stuffed Grape Leaves

Ingredients

- 1 Servings
- 40 Preserved grape leaves
- 1 cup Rice
- 1/2 lb Ground lamb
- 1 1/2 tsp Salt
- 1/2 tsp Pepper
- 1/4 tsp Allspice
- 1/4 tsp Cinnamon
- 2 Tsp Vegetable oil
- 1/4 cup Fresh lemon juice
- 1 Water

Preparation

- This traditional Middle Eastern dish is a lot of work. However, once you get the hang of the rolling technique it gets easier.
- The combination of the slightly acidic leaf, rice and meat stuffing, and the cool yogurt make it worth it.
- If you can get your hands on fresh grape leaves, by all means use them. Just remember to soften them up by soaking them in hot water for 10 minutes.
- Remove preserved grape leaves from jar and rinse with water. Set aside. In a medium bowl, mix rice ground lamb, salt, pepper, allspice, cinnamon, and vegetable oil.
- Place a heaping teaspoonful of rice mixture on dull side of grape leaf. Begin rolling in a jelly roll fashion.
- After the first roll, tuck in the ends, and continue rolling. The roll should be firm, but not too tight so that the expanding rice won't burst it and not too loose so it won't sag and the filling won't ooze out.
- Repeat with the rest of the leaves and the filling. In a 2 1/2 quart pan, arrange rolls in compact rows. Add enough water to just below the top row of rolls.
- Place a small plate on top of the rolls. This is to weigh them down so they will remain intact while they cook. Bring the pot to a boil, reduce heat.
- Cover and let simmer until leaves are tender (45 minutes). Most of the water should have evaporated at this point.
- Uncover, add lemon juice and cook for 5 minutes longer. Remove from heat and transfer to serving platter. Serve with yogurt.

Sfeeha

(Baked Lamb Pies)

Ingredients
- DOUGH
- 2 3/4 cups Lukewarm water
- 2 pkg Active dry yeast
- 1 pinch Sugar
- 8 cups All purpose flour
- 2 tsp Salt
- 1/4 cup Olive oil
- FILLING
- 2 cups Finely chopped onion
- 2 tsp Salt
- 4 Tsp Olive oil
- 1/2 cup Pine nuts (pignolia)
- 2 lb Lean boneless lamb
- 2 med Fresh, ripe, peeled, seeded and finely chopped tomato
- 1/2 cup Finely chopped green pepper
- 1/2 cup Finely chopped flat leaf parsley parsley
- 1/2 cup Fresh lemon juice
- 1/4 cup Red wine vinegar
- 1 Tsp Tomato paste
- 1 tsp Cayenne pepper
- 1 tsp Allspice
- 2 tsp Salt
- 1 Freshly ground black pepper

Preparation
- Make the dough in the following fashion: pour 1/4 cup of the lukewarm water into a small, shallow bowl and sprinkle it with the yeast and sugar.
- Let the mixture rest for 2 or 3 minutes, and then stir to dissolve the yeast completely. Set the bowl in a warm, draft free place (such as a turned off oven) for about 5 minutes, or until the mixture almost doubles in volume.
- In a deep mixing bowl, combine the flour and the 2 teaspoons of salt, make a well in the center and into it pour the yeast mixture, the 1/4 cup of olive oil, and 2 cups of the remaining lukewarm water.
- Gently stir the center ingredients together with a large spoon, then slowly incorporate the flour and continue to beat until the ingredients are well combined.
- Add up to 1/2 cup more lukewarm water, beating it in a tablespoon or so at a time, and using as much as necessary to form a dough that can be gathered into a compact ball.
- If the dough is difficult to stir, work in the water with your fingers. Place the dough on a lightly floured surface and knead it by pressing it down,

- pushing it forward several times with the heel of your hand and folding it back on itself.
- Repeat for about 20 minutes, or until the dough is smooth and elastic. Sprinkle it from time to time with a little flour to prevent it from sticking to the board.
- Shape the dough into a ball and place it in a lightly oiled bowl. Drape loosely with a kitchen towel and set aside in the warm, draft free place for 45 minutes to 1 hour, or until the dough doubles in bulk.
- Punch the dough down with a single blow of your fist and divide it into 16 equal pieces. Roll each piece into a ball about 1 ½ inches in diameter, cover the balls with a towel and let them rest for 30 minutes.
- FILLING:
- Meanwhile, prepare the filling. Drop the onions into a deep bowl and sprinkle them with 1 tablespoon of the salt, turning them about with a spoon to coat them evenly.
- Let the onions rest at room temperature for at least 30 minutes, then squeeze them dry and return them to the bowl. In a small skillet or saucepan, heat 1 tablespoon of olive oil until a light haze forms above it.
- Add the pine nuts and, stirring constantly, brown them lightly. Add them to the bowl of onions, along with the lamb, tomatoes, green pepper, parsley, lemon juice, vinegar, tomato paste, cayenne pepper, allspice, 2 teaspoons of salt and a liberal grinding of black pepper.
- Knead the mixture vigorously with both hands, then beat with a wooden spoon until the mixture is smooth and fluffy. Taste for seasoning.
- Preheat the oven to 500 degrees (F). With a pastry brush, coat 3 large baking sheets or jelly roll pans with the remaining 3 tablespoons of oil.
- On a lightly floured surface, roll each of the balls into a round about 4 inches in diameter and no more than 1/8 inch thick. To make open face pies, spoon about 1/2 cup of the lamb filling mixture on the center of each round.
- Then with a spatula or the back of the spoon, spread the filling to about 1/2 inch of the edge. To make closed pies, spoon about 1/2 cup of the filling on the center of each round.
- Pull up the edge from 3 equally distant points to make a roughly triangular shaped pie and pinch the dough securely together at the top. With a metal spatula, arrange the pies on the baking sheets.
- Bake in the lower third of the oven for 30 minutes, or until the pastry is lightly browned. Serve hot, or at room temperature, accompanied, if you like, with yogurt.
- Milk. Decorate with pine nuts place at 1 1/2-2 inch intervals.
- Bake at 350 deg. F for 30- 35 minutes, until crust becomes light brown and a toothpick inserted in the middle pulls out clean. Cool, Cut into 40 squares with a pine nuts in each center

Reshmi Kabab

Ingredients
- 1 Kg Boneless chicken
- 4 med Sized onions
- 8 Cloves garlic
- 1 bunch Coriander (cilantro) leaves
- 1 tsp Cumin (jeera) seeds
- 1 To Taste white pepper
- 1 tsp Garam masala (available in 1 Indian stores)
- 2 Eggs
- 1 To Taste salt
- 1 Lemon
- 1 Spring onion (red onions 1are ok)
- 1 Ginger

Preparation
- Mince the chicken. Grind all ingredients together except eggs and salt. Mix in the eggs and salt.
- Shape into sausages, put on skewers and cook over charcoal fire or in rotisserie till tender. Garnish with onions and lemon.

Persian Quince Stew
(Khoresh-E Beh)

Ingredients
- 2 Finely sliced onion
- 1/3 cup Oil (or butter)
- 1 lb stewing meat (lamb (or beef) cut in 1 inch cubes
- 1 tsp Salt
- 1/4 tsp Pepper
- 1/2 tsp Ground cinnamon
- 3 cups Water
- 2 lg Quinces
- 3 Tsp Sugar
- 1/4 cup Vinegar (or lemon juice)
- 1/4 tsp Ground saffron, dissolved in 1 Tsp hot water
- 1/3 cup Yellow split peas
- CHELO
- 3 cups Basmati rice

- 8 cups Water
- 2 Tsp Salt
- 3/4 cup Melted butter
- 1/2 t saffron, dissolved in 2T ,water, hot
- 2 Tsp Yogurt (opt)

Preparation

- In large pot, brown onions in 3 Tbsp. of oil or butter. Add meat and brown. Add salt, pepper, and cinnamon. Add water, cover and simmer over low heat for 1 hr, stirring occasionally.
- Wash, but don't peel quinces. Use apple corer to remove seeds. Slice as for apple pie. In skillet, sauté in 2 Tbsp. oil or butter and set aside.
- To the meat, add sugar, vinegar or lemon juice, saffron, split peas, and quince. Cover and simmer 35 minutes. Check to see that meat and fruit are cooked.
- Taste and correct seasoning. Transfer to deep casserole dish and keep in warm oven until ready to serve. Serve hot with chelo (recipe below.) Chelo:
- Wash rice 5 times in cold water. Bring water and salt to boil in a large non-stick pan. Add washed and drained rice.
- Boil 6 minutes, stirring gently twice to loosen grains that may have stuck to bottom. Drain rice in colander and rinse in lukewarm water.
- In same pot, heat half the butter, 2 Tbsp. hot water, a drop of dissolved saffron, and yogurt. Taking one spatula at a time, place rice gently in pot mounding in the shape of a pyramid.
- Dissolve remaining butter in 2 Tbsp. hot water and pour over rice. Place clean dishtowel over pot and cover firmly with lid to prevent steam from escaping.
- Cook 10 minutes over medium heat and 50 minutes over low heat. Remove from heat. Allow to cool 5 minutes on a damp surface without removing lid.
- Put 2 Tbsp. of the rice in with remaining saffron and set aside for garnish. Gently remove rice from pot without disturbing crust. Sprinkle saffron flavored rice over top and serve. Detach crust and serve separately.

Persian Abgusht

Ingredients

- 1 lb Stew meat (beef or lamb)
- 1 lg Onion (chopped)
- 1 To Taste salt and pepper
- 1/2 tsp Turmeric
- 1/2 tsp Saffron

- 2 Large potatoes
- 1/2 cup Chick peas
- 2 Tomatoes
- 1 Chopped eggplant (optional)
- 1 Water

Preparation

- Put everything in a large pot and simmer for 1-1/2 to 2 hours on a low setting. Add salt and pepper to taste and any other favorite soup flavorings.
- Make sure there is plenty of water. When done, the water will have the consistency of a thick soup and the other ingredients will be well cooked.
- Beat with large spoon until light and fluffy.
- Beat in 1/4 cup of the flour and when it is completely absorbed, add the egg. Beating well after each addition, add 1 cup of flour, then 2 tablespoons of the milk and vanilla mixture, followed by another cup of flour, the rest of the milk mixture and all of the remaining flour.
- Gather the dough into a ball, cover it with wax paper or plastic wrap and refrigerate for at least 30 minutes. To make the cookies, preheat the oven to 350 degrees (F).
- With a pastry brush, coat 2 large baking sheets with the remaining 2 tablespoons of softened butter. On a lightly floured surface, roll the dough out into a rough circle about 1/16 inches thick.
- With a 4 to 5 inch round cookie cutter (or pastry wheel), cut the dough into a many rounds as you can. Then gather the scraps into a small ball, reroll and cut into similar rounds, continuing the process until all the dough has been used.
- Oznei haman is traditionally shaped like three cornered hats. To form each one, place a heaping tablespoon of the poppy seed filling in the center of a round under the nearest edge in such a way the thumbs and index.
- Fingers will form a triangle when they are brought up over the filling until they meet above it. Pinch the top together tightly to enclose the filling completely.
- Place the cookies on the baking sheets, brush the tops with the beaten egg yolk and milk mixture and bake in the center of the oven for 20 to 25 minutes, or until they are lightly browned.
- With a spatula, transfer them to a cake rack to cool before serving.

###

Part 11: Morocco Recipes

The strong Arab influence found in two of the royal cities, Fez and Marrakech, contributed greatly to Moroccan cuisine, as did the Andalusian sensibilities of Tetuan and the Jewish traditions from the coastal city of Essaouira. Aspects of all of these cultures can be found in four of the best-loved Moroccan dishes: couscous, plumped semolina grains which are served with a variety of toppings; bisteeya, a delectable three-layer pie which is both savory and sweet and wrapped in the thinnest of pastry; mechoui, tender roasted lamb; and djej emshmel, succulent roasted chicken cooked with olives and lemon.

The Moroccans are quick to point out that the best meals are found not in the restaurants but in the homes.

Moroccan Almond Rolls

Ingredients

- 2 1/4 cups Unbleached all-purpose flour- (sifted)
- 1 cup Butter
- 1/2 tsp Salt ice water

FILLING

- 8 oz Almond paste
- 1 lg Egg
- 2 Tsp Sugar
- 1/3 cup Ground almonds

Preparation

- Place the flour, butter and salt in a mixing bowl. Cut in the butter with a pastry blender until the mixture is crumbly. Add the ice water and blend well with a fork, until moistened.
- Shape into a ball and divide it into 3 sections, wrap, and refrigerate for at least 1 hour, (no more than 2 hours). Meanwhile, prepare the filling by mixing all of the ingredients together.
- Remove the dough from the refrigerator, and roll out 1 section into a 12 X 12-inch square. Cut into 3-inch squares. Place a small piece of filling at one corner of each small square and roll up, diagonally.
- Repeat with the remaining two sections of dough. Place the rolled squares on ungreased cookie sheets and bake in a preheated 400 Degree F. oven for 10 to 12 minutes.

Moroccan Anise Bread

Ingredients

- 1 Tsp Active dry yeast
- 1 1/3 cups Warm water
- 1 tsp Sugar (or honey)
- 1 Tsp Vegetable oil
- 2 1/2 tsp Anise seeds
- 2 tsp Table salt or
- 4 tsp Kosher salt
- 4 cups Unbleached all-purpose flour
- 1 Beaten egg white with
- 1 tsp Water
- Tsp Sesame seeds

Preparation

- Dissolve the yeast in 1/4 cup of the water. Add the sugar or honey and let stand until foamy, 5 to 10 minutes. Add the remaining water, oil, anise, salt, and 2 cups of the flour.
- Gradually stir in the remaining flour until the mixture holds together. On a lightly floured surface, knead the dough until smooth and elastic, about 10 minutes. Place in a greased bowl, turning to coat.
- Cover loosely with a towel or plastic wrap and let rise at room temperature until double in bulk, about 1-1/2 hours, or Punch down the dough and divide in half. Shape each piece into a ball, cover, and let rest for about 10 minutes.
- Sprinkle a large baking sheet with cornmeal or fine semolina or grease the baking sheet. Flatten each dough ball into a 6-inch round. Some cooks flute the outer edge, others leave it plain.
- Place the rounds on the prepared baking sheet, cover, and let Preheat the oven to 375 degrees. Prick the dough around the sides with the tines of a fork or a toothpick. Brush the tops of the loaves with the egg white and lightly sprinkle with the sesame seeds.
- Bake until golden brown and hollow-sounding when tapped, about 30 minutes. Transfer to a wire rack to cool.

Moroccan Beef Kefta
(On Skewers with Chopped Vegetable Salad)

Ingredients

- 1 1/2 lb Ground beef
- 1/2 cup Grated onion
- 2 Cloves garlic -- finely minced
- 2 Tsp Chopped parsley finely fresh
- 2 Tsp Chopped coriander finely fresh
- 3 tsp Chopped finely fresh mint
- 2 tsp Chopped marjoram finely fresh
- 1/2 tsp Ground cumin
- 1/2 tsp Paprika
- 1/4 tsp Cayenne
- 1 Chopped vegetable salad
- 1 Peeled seedless cucumber
- 1 lg Tomato -- seeded and finely
- 1 Green bell pepper -- seeded
- 1 And finely

- 1 Hot Italian-style pepper --
- 1 Seeded and finely
- 2 Cloves garlic -- finely
- 1 Minced
- 3 Tsp Chopped finely fresh mint
- 2 Tsp Red wine vinegar
- 2 Tsp Olive oil -- (up to 3)
- 1 Dried mint
- 1 tsp Dried marjoram

Preparation

- In a large bowl combine the beef, onion, garlic, parsley, coriander, mint, marjoram, salt, pepper, cumin, paprika and cayenne. Cover and let sit for one hour. Soak 12 wooden skewers in water for one hour.
- In a separate bowl combine cucumber, tomato, bell pepper, hot pepper, garlic, mint, red wine vinegar, olive oil, salt and pepper tossing to combine. Cover and let marinate at room temperature until ready to serve. Preheat grill or broiler.
- Dip hands into a bowl of water. Shape and pack about a 1/3 cup of the meat mixture into 2 sausage-shapes on a soaked wooden skewer. Repeat procedure for remaining meat and skewers.
- Grill the keftas on both sides until cooked through, about 3 to 4 minutes per side. Serve hot with chopped salad.

Moroccan Beef Stew

Ingredients

- 8 Servings
- 2 lb Chuck roast (bite-size)
- 1/4 tsp Cumin
- 3 Tsp Flour
- 1/4 tsp Ginger
- 2 tsp Salt
- 1/8 tsp Cayenne pepper
- 2 Tsp Vegetable oil
- 1 cup Chopped celery
- 20 oz Pineapple chunks
- 1/2 cup Chopped onion
- 2 cups Juice/water
- 2 Minced cloves garlic
- 1/2 tsp Paprika
- 1 cup Sliced carrots

- 1/4 tsp Coriander
- 3 sm Wedged tomatoes
- 1/4 tsp Turmeric parsley flakes

Preparation
- Dredge beef in flour and salt and brown in oil. Pour off drippings. Add spices, celery, onion and garlic. Stir in juice and water. Cook slowly 1 hour. Add carrots and cook 30 minutes more. Add pineapple and tomatoes and heat through. Garning with parsley. Makes 8 servings.

Moroccan Bread

Ingredients
- 2 Tsp Baking yeast
- 1 tsp Honey
- 1/2 cup Warm water
- 8 1/2 cups Whole wheat flour
- 2 Tsp Anise seed
- 2 tsp Sesame seeds
- 1 tsp Salt
- 1 cup Warm milk
- 2 cups Warm water (approximately)
- 1 Corn meal

Preparation
- Combine first 3 ingredients in a small bowl and allow to sit 2 to 3 minutes till yeast dissolves. Stir and set aside on counter in a warm place and allow to rise till mixture is bubbly and doubles in volume.
- In the meantime, mix the next 4 ingredients together in a mixing bowl and heat milk to lukewarm. Make a crater in the middle of the flour and pour in the risen, bubbly yeast mixture and the warm milk and mix in.
- Add the warm water a little at a time to form stiff dough (you may need a little more or less than 2 cups of water depending on variety of whole wheat flour used, humidity, etc.) Turn dough onto a lightly floured surface and knead for 10 to 15 minutes.
- The dough should be so stiff that it needs to be kneaded with fists. Divide dough into quarters and roll each piece into a ball. Allow to sit on floured surface about 5 minutes. In the meantime, sprinkle 2 cookie sheets with corn meal.
- Form each ball of dough into a large cone shape. Place 2 cones on each cookie sheet and flatten each into round loaves that are slightly raised in the centers, about 6" in diameter.
- Cover loaves with plastic wrap and allow to rise about 2 hours in a warm place. Preheat oven to 400 F degrees. Just before baking, gently prick

bread around the sides in 4 places and bake at 400 F degrees for 12 minutes.
- Turn heat down to 300 F degrees and bake another 30 to 40 minutes till bread sounds hollow when tapped on the bottom. Remove from oven and allow to cool.

Moroccan Brisket With Olives

Ingredients
- 6 lb Brisket of beef
- 1 Lamb can be substituted
- 2 cloves peeled and halved garlic
- 1/4 cup Olive oil
- 1/4 tsp Tumeric
- 1 or 1   A few strands saffron
- 1 tsp fresh grated ginger
- 2 lg Diced Spanish onions
- 4 Tsp chopped with celery
- 1 sm peeled sliced in carrot
- Paper thin rounds
- 1 lb Green olives
- 2lg Peeled and diced tomatoes
- 1or 16 oz Canned stewed tomatoes
- 1 Lemon for juice

Preparation
- Sprinkle meat with salt and pepper; rub with garlic. In a heavy roasting pan, sear meat on all sides in a bit of olive oil. Remove and set aside. In same pot, add remaining olive oil, turmeric (or saffron), ginger, and onions.
- Sauté until onions are limp. Add celery and carrots. Sauté a bit more. Add tomatoes and mix. Remove 1/3 of the mixture and placed seared meat on the remainder. Cover with the rest of the mixture.
- Cover, and bake in pre-heated over at 350 degrees F until meat is tender about 3 hours). Remove, and refrigerate. In the meantime, pit the olives. Place olives in a pot. Cover with water and bring to a boil.
- Drain, and repeat the process. (to remove saltiness of the olives). Remove brisket from refrigerator. Remove any fat that may have collected. Slice the meat against the grain.
- Return meat to a heavy pot with the mixture. Sprinkle the olives over the meat. Reheat at 350 deg F for 1/2 hour, and serve.

Moroccan Charosets

Ingredients
- 2 cups Pitted dates
- 1/2 cup Golden raisins
- 1/2 cup Dark raisins
- 1/2 cup Walnuts
- 2 Tsp Sweet Passover red wine

Preparation
- Process dates, raisins and walnuts in food processor until mixture is finely chopped and begins to mass. Add enough wine to make sticky dough. Line baking sheet with waxed paper.
- Drop mixture by slightly rounded measuring teaspoonfuls onto pan. Roll with moistened palms into hazelnut-size balls. Refrigerate for at least 3 hours or until firm.

Moroccan Chick Pea Soup

Ingredients
- 2 Tsp Safflower oil
- 2 Grated carrots
- 2 Minced cloves garlic
- 1 Chop fine (1/2 c) med onion
- 15 oz Rinse drain can chick peas
- 3 cups Vegetable stock
- 1/3 cup Tahini
- 2 Tsp Lemon juice
- 1 Tsp Chopped fresh parsley
- 3/4 tsp Ground cumin
- 1/2 tsp Black pepper
- 1/2 tsp Thyme leaves
- 1/4 tsp Powdered turmeric
- 1/8 tsp Cayenne pepper

Preparation
- GARNISH: toasted sesame seeds, minced scallions, finely chopped tomatoes, or Herbed Garlic Croutons, optional in 4-5 qt saucepan, heat oil. Add carrots, garlic, and onion; cook until tender. Set aside.
- Meanwhile, in food processor, puree chick peas, 1 cup of vegetable stock, tahini, and lemon juice. Stir pureed mixture into saucepan. Add remaining ingredients including vegetable stock.

- Cover and cook for 5 minutes to heat through. Top with garnish if desired. VARIATIONS: -substitute olive oil for safflower oil- add 1 med sweet red pepper, finely chopped; sauté with other veggies.

Moroccan Chicken

Ingredients
- 3 lb Cut into serving-pieces chicken
- 4 Split chicken breasts
- 8 Snipped dried figs
- 1 8-oz Can tomato sauce
- 1/2 cup chopped onion
- 2 cloves minced garlic
- 1/4 cup White wine (or apple juice)
- 2 Bay leaves
- 1/2 tsp Ground allspice
- 1 tsp Dried thyme leaves
- 1/2 cup chopped-optional green pepper
- 2 Tsp Sesame
- 2 Tsp slivered almonds

Preparation
- Skin chicken. Place in a pot or hearty skillet. Add remaining ingredients, except sesame seeds or almonds. Cover and cook in a slow cooker about 6 hours or cook in oven on low heat about 2 hours.
- For faster cooking, bring to a boil on top of range, reduce heat to low, and cook for 20-35 minutes depending on thickness of chicken pieces. Sprinkle sesame seeds or almonds on top before serving. This makes six 3-oz servings.

Moroccan Chicken with Olives

Ingredients
- 1/4 cup Cilantro
- 1 Tsp Paprika
- 2 tsp Cumin
- 1/2 tsp Salt
- 1/2 tsp Turmeric
- 1/2 tsp Ginger
- 2 Cloves garlic

- 1/2 lb Cut up chicken
- 1/3 cup Flour
- 1/2 cup Water
- 1/4 cup Lemon juice
- 1 tsp Chicken bouillon
- 1/2 cup Kalamata (or Greek olives)
- 1 Sliced lemon

Preparation
- Mix cilantro, paprika, cumin, salt, turmeric, ginger and garlic. Rub mixture on all sides of chicken. Coat with flour. Place chicken in ungreased 13x9x2 inch baking dish. Mix water, lemon juice and bouillon. Pour over chicken.
- Add olives and lemon slices. Cook uncovered at 350 degrees spooning juices over chicken occasionally, until thickest pieces of chicken are done, about 1 hour. Serve with couscous or rice if desired

Moroccan Chicken Casserole

Ingredients
- 1 large Whole chicken cut into 4 pieces
- 100 ml Olive oil
- A few springs of thyme
- 500 gms Sliced lengthways of salad potatoes
- 6 Halved shallots
- 2 Tbsp Butter
- 150 gms Stoned black olives
- 1 Lemon zest
- 2 Tbsp White wine
- 3 Bay leaves
- 2 Tbsp Chopped parsley
- 1 ½ Tbsp Paprika
- 150 g Cherry tomatoes
- 1 tsp Cumin
- 1 Dried red chili pepper
- Salt & pepper
- 1 Big bowl
- 1 Frying pan
- 1 Casserole dish
- 1 Small pot
- 1 Colander
- 1 Spoon
- 1 Knife

Preparation

- Preheat the oven: Start by turning the oven to 200°C. Season the chicken: Rub the chicken with 1-2 tbsp of olive oil and season with salt and pepper. Par boils the potatoes:
- In a small pot cover the potatoes with water, place on the heat and bring to a boil. Once boiling cook for 3 minutes. Take off the heat, drain and put aside.
- Prepare the chicken: Heat a heavy skillet or frying pan and add 2 tbsp of olive oil. Once heated up, place the chicken quarters in the pan skin side down, brown them and then add the shallots and garlic until all lightly browned.
- Add the potatoes and cook until lightly browned. Put the lemon zest in a pot of cold water and bring to a boil for 3 minutes. Combine the ingredients together: Put the chicken and potatoes into a big bowl.
- Next, add to the bowl all the remaining ingredients, except the parsley. Mix the ingredients: Make sure your hands are properly washed and mix all the ingredients together.
- Place all in dish: Using a casserole dish large enough to hold all the ingredients, pour in the mixture. Put in the oven: Place the dish in the oven and cook for 1 hour and 15 minutes at 200°C.
- Baste the chicken: Baste the casserole occasionally during the cooking time to keep the chicken covered with the juices, you can add about half a cup of water if there are not enough juices. Serve and enjoy: When cooked thoroughly, take the casserole out of the oven and serve with freshly chopped parsley.

Moroccan Date Cake

Ingredients

- 1/2 cup Butter
- 1/4 cup Sugar (up to 1/2 cup)
- 4 Eggs
- 1 tsp Baking powder
- 1 cup Unbleached white flour
- 1 tsp Cinnamon
- 1 tsp Nutmeg
- 1/2 tsp Ground cloves
- 1/2 cup Milk
- 1/2 tsp Pure vanilla extract
- 1 cup Chopped pitted dates
- 1 Fresh whipped cream

Preparation

- Preheat the oven to 325 F. Cream together the butter and sugar. Beat in the eggs. Combine the baking powder, flour, cinnamon, nutmeg, and cloves. Add the dry ingredients to the egg mixture, beating well.
- Mix in the milk and vanilla. Beat well. Add the chopped dates and walnuts and stir again to distribute them evenly. Butter and flour a 9-inch cake pan.
- Pour the batter into the pan. Bake for about 30 minutes, until a knife inserted into the center comes out clean. Serve with fresh whipped cream.

Moroccan Five-Grain Pilaf

Ingredients

- 1 Tsp Olive oil
- 1 lg Chopped onion
- 1 Tsp Finely-chopped ginger root
- 1 Minced clove garlic
- 2 tsp Curry powder
- 1 tsp Ground cumin
- 1/2 tsp Cinnamon
- 1/2 tsp Ground turmeric
- 1/2 cups Vegetable stock (or chicken)
- 1 Stock
- 1/2 cup Long grain brown rice
- 1/2 cup Wheat berries
- 1/2 cup Pearl barley
- 1/2 cup Quinoa
- 1/2 cup Millet
- 1 tsp Salt
- 2 Cut in 1/2-inch carrots
- 1 Cubes
- 19 oz Drained and can garbanzos
- 1 Rinsed
- 1 bunch Spinach (or Swiss chard)
- 1 Sliced thinly
- 1/4 cup Almonds (or pine nuts)-Slivered
- 1 Toasted (optional)

Preparation

- Heat oil in a large saucepan over medium heat. Stir in the onion, ginger and garlic; cook, stirring, about 4 minutes or until softened. Add curry

powder, cumin, cinnamon and turmeric; cook one minute.
- Stir in the stock, rice, wheat berries, barley and salt. Bring to a boil, reduce heat and simmer, covered, for 30 minutes. Place quinoa in sieve; rinse well under running water. Add to saucepan with millet and carrots.
- Cover; simmer about 20 minutes or until liquid is almost absorbed. Place garbanzos and spinach (or Swiss chard) on top of grains in saucepan, without stirring.
- Replace cover; cook about 5 minutes longer or until spinach is just wilted and liquid is absorbed. Toss with a fork; transfer to a large bowl or platter. Sprinkle with nuts.

###

Part 12: Philippines Recipes

Filipino cuisine *is a blend of the exotic and familiar. Just as the Filipino people are part Malay, Chinese and Spanish, so is the cooking of the Philippines. And more recently other cultures have influenced Filipino food. These influences have come from the Americans, Japanese, and Germans.*

Spanish additions to the Filipino cuisine predominate. It has been said that about 80 percent of the dishes prepared in the Philippines today can be traced to Spain.

The Spaniards introduced tomatoes and garlic along with the technique of sautéing them with onions in olive oil.

Banana Blossom Ginataan

Ingredients
- 2 Banana blossoms
- 1 The ones in the can,10 oz
- 1 Drained
- 1 cup Pure coconut milk
- 2 Tsp Vinegar (if using 5% acidity try 1:1 vinegar/water)
- 1/4cup Sliced tomatoes
- 1/4cup Sliced onion
- Crushed garlic cloves
- 1 Tsp Vegetable oil
- Dried red chilies
- 1 tsp Salt and pepper

Preparation
- If using fresh pusong saging (banana blossoms): remove the tough covering of the blossoms. Slice thin crosswise. Add 2 tbsp salt and squeeze off bitter juice. Rinse in water and squeeze dry. Set aside.
- If using canned pusong saging: drain, rinse then drain again. Slice thin crosswise. Set aside
- Heat oil in skillet, if using dried red chilies, add them when the oil is hot but not smoking and let the skins darken somewhat before you add the garlic. Sauté garlic until light brown
- Add onion, fry till translucent, and then add tomatoes. Cook for around 3 minutes. Add banana blossoms and vinegar/water mixture and then bring to boil without stirring. Simmer for around 3 minutes.
- Add salt and pepper to taste and stir. Continue to cook until banana blossom is tender. Add pure coconut cream and remove from heat. Let stand for a few minutes to help develop the flavors.

Banana Ketchup

Ingredients

- ½ cup Golden raisins
- 1/3 cup Chopped onions coarsely
- 21 gms Garlic cloves
- 1/3 cup Tomato paste
- 1 1/3 cups Cider vinegar
- 4 lg Very ripe peeled bananas-and cut into chunk
- 4 cups Water
- 1/2 cup packed dark brown sugar,
- 1 1/2 tsp Salt
- 1/2 tsp Cayenne pepper
- 1/4 cup light corn syrup
- 2 tsp Ground allspice
- 3/4 tsp Ground cinnamon
- 3/4 tsp Freshly grated nutmeg
- 1/2 tsp Freshly ground black pepper
- 1/4 tsp Ground cloves
- 2 Tsp dark rum

Preparation

- Combine the raisins, onions, garlic, tomato paste and 1/3 cup vinegar in the container of a food processor, Process the mixture until smooth. Transfer the mixture to a large, heavy saucepan.
- Add the banana chunks and 1/3 cup vinegar to the food processor container. Process the mixture until smooth. Transfer the banana mixture to the saucepan.
- Add the remaining 2/3 cup vinegar, 3 cups water, brown sugar, salt and cayenne pepper. Bring the mixture in the saucepan to a boil over medium-high heat, stirring frequently.
- Reduce the heat to low and cook the ketchup, uncovered, stirring occasionally, for 1 1/4 hours. If the ketchup threatens to stick to the bottom of the pan at any point.
- Add some of the remaining water, up to 1 cup. Add the corn syrup, allspice, cinnamon, nutmeg, pepper and cloves to the ketchup.
- Cook the ketchup over medium-low heat, stirring frequently, for 15 minutes longer, or until it is thick enough to coat a metal spoon. Stir in the rum.
- Remove the ketchup from the heat and let it cool few minutes. Force the ketchup through a fine sieve to strain it, pressing down hard on the solids.
- Remove the ketchup from the heat and let it cool to room temperature. Store the banana ketchup, covered in the refrigerator for up to 1 month. Makes about 3 1/2 cups.

Banana Peanut Salad

Ingredients
- Medium-sized ripe bananas
- 16 Tsp Chopped peanuts
- Mayonnaise
- Lettuce

Preparation
- Slice crosswise and thin 2 bananas for each individual serving and mix with two tablespoons chopped peanuts. Add mayonnaise, mix lightly with a fork and arrange on lettuce leaves before serving.

Basic Adobo

Ingredients
- 3 lb Chicken thighs or
- 3 lb Pork butt
- 1/2cup Vinegar
- 1/4cup Soy sauce garlic cloves
- 1/4 tsp Salt
- 1/4 tsp Crushed peppercorns
- Crushed bay leaf

Preparation
- Cut chicken pieces in half if thighs are large. If using pork, cut pork into 1 1/2 inch pieces. In a saucepan, combine all ingredients. Let stand for 1 to 3 hours.
- Bring to a boil Cover, lower heat, and simmer for 30 minutes (45 minutes for pork). Remove cover and simmer 15 more minutes or until liquid evaporates and chicken or pork is lightly browned. Makes six

Bibinka
(Philippine Dessert)

Ingredients
- 4cups Divided fresh coconut milk
- 1 1/2cups Divided brown sugar

- 1 1/3 cups Mocha rice
- Wilted banana leaves

Preparation

- Reserve 1/2 cup coconut milk & 1/2 cup brown sugar for topping. Wash rice & let stand in cold water (while cooking coconut milk).
- Cook 3-1/2 cups coconut milk in top of double boiler for 30 minutes, stirring constantly. Note: Keep water in lower portion at constant boil.
- Add 1 cup brown sugar. Drain mocha rice in strainer and stir into milk mixture. Cook in double boiler for 30 minutes or until thick. Stirring constantly.
- Line baking pan with banana leaves and pour in pudding. Sprinkle top with mixture of 1/2 cup brown sugar and 1/2 cup coconut milk.
- Bake in oven set at 350F for 5 minutes then lower temperature to 300F and continue baking for 30 minutes. Cool in pan & cut in 3inches squares.

Calderetta

Ingredients

- 1 ½ lb. beef round cubed
- 1/4 Cup vinegar
- Crushed peppercorns
- 1 tsp salt
- 2 Cup crushed garlic
- 1/4 Cup oil
- 1 Cup Sliced onion,
- 1/2 Cup tomato sauce
- 2 Cup Boiling water
- 1 Cup red (or green pepper) strips
- 1 bay leaf
- 1 dash of hot sauce
- 1/3 Cup liver spread

Preparation

- Marinate beef in mixture of vinegar, peppercorn, and salt and crushed garlic for 1 1/2 - 2 hours. Fry pieces of beef in cooking oil.
- Add onions and sauté until tender. Pour in tomato sauce and boiling water.
- Add the green pepper, bay leaf and hot sauce as desired. Cover and simmer until meat is tender. Blend in liver spread. Cook 5 minutes more.

Cari-Cari De Pata Y Rabo

Ingredients

- 1 ox tail (buntot ng baka)
- 1 ox shin (pata ng baka)
- 6 Cups water
- 1/2 Cup atchuete seeds
- 1/2 Cup hot water
- Long egg plants
- 400 gms snake beans (sitao)
- 1 banana flower
- 1 chopped garlic head,
- 2medium Sliced onions,
- 1/4 Cup cooking oil
- 1/2 Cup fermented shrimp paste
- 1 Cup ground peanuts
- 1 Cup toasted & ground rice,
- 1 salt and msg to taste
- 1 Bagoong guisado
- 1/4 Cup cooking oil
- 1 Chopped garlic head,
- 1/4 Kg diced boiled pork,
- 1 tsp sugar
- 1 1/2 Cup bagoong alamang
- 1/4 Cup native vinegar
- 1/4 Cup pork broth

Preparation

- Boil the buntot and pata in water until tender. Cut into desired pieces and set aside. Soak atsuete seeds in hot water. Rub to bring out color. Set aside.
- Cut vegetables into desired pieces. Boil water, drop sitao and parboil. Remove, set aside. Do likewise with eggplants and puso ng saging. Sauté garlic and onions in cooking oil.
- Add bagoong and atsuete water. Let boil 5 minutes. Blend in ground peanuts and ground rice. Bring to a boil then put in the meats.
- Just before removing from the fire, add the vegetables. Serve with Bagoong Guisado. Bagoong Guisado preparation. Sauté garlic and onion in cooking oil.
- Add the pork, bagoong and sugar. Blend well, and then add vinegar and

broth. Boil until quite dry. Serve with the Cari-Cari.

Casa Manila's Pork Adobo

Ingredients
- 4 lb Trimmed of pork roast
- 1 Bone and cubed fat
- 1 Cup vinegar
- 1/4 Cup soy sauce
- 4 Crushed garlic cloves
- 2 tsp sugar
- 1 tsp salt
- 1/2 tsp pepper, Freshly Ground

Preparation
- In bowl, combine pork, vinegar, soy sauce, garlic, sugar, salt and pepper; marinate 30 minutes.
- Transfer to heavy bottomed skillet; bring to a boil; reduce heat, simmer 3 1/2 to 4 hours or until liquids almost evaporated. Serve with steamed rice.

Eva's Lumpia

Ingredients
- 2 Tsp oil
- 1 med diced onion
- 1 clove minced garlic,
- 1 lg pared and diced potato
- 1 tsp salt
- 1/2 Cup diced carrots
- 1/4 tsp pepper
- 1/2 Cup French cut green beans
- 2 Tsp soy sauce
- 1/2 cup shredded cabbage
- ¼ lb diced pork
- 1 ground pork (or),Ground
- 1 Beef (basically any meat will work, even chicken)

Preparation
- If you prefer you can add 1/4 lb. shrimp, diced. Also if you like you can

put 1/2 cup of bean sprouts
- Heat oil, sauté garlic and onion. Add pork, sauté until fully cooked, drain. Add water, cover and simmer 10 to 15 min. Season with salt, pepper, and soy sauce.
- Add potato and carrots, sauté for 5 min. Add green beans and cabbage (this would be the time to add the shrimp and bean sprouts if you were to use them).
- Cook stirring 5-10 min. or until vegetables are done. Let cool to room temperature. Wrap filling in Lumpia wrappers. Fry in about 1 inch of hot oil, a couple of minutes on each side, until light golden brown.

Filipino Breakfast Steaks

Ingredients
- 2 1/4 lb sliced sirloin, 1/8 to¼ lb.
- 1 Inch thick
- 1 1/2 Tsp salt
- 2 Tsp brown sugar
- 1 tsp chopped garlic -- finely,
- 1/2 t Cracked black pepper

Preparation
- Combine salt, sugar, garlic, and black pepper. Spread rub evenly on both sides of meat and store covered (or in a plastic bag) in the refrigerator overnight.
- Sun dry a couple of hours before cooking in smoker to medium or medium well. Serving Suggestions: Serve with a salsa of chopped fresh tomatoes, chopped onions, grated radish, chopped fresh cilantro, oriental fish sauce (or salt) to taste, crushed hot chilies, and a little vinegar(or lemon juice).
- For heavy eaters, chop meat into small pieces and serve sprinkled over a mound of garlic fried rice and fried eggs.

Fresh Lumpia

Ingredients
- 1 lb Browned and fat- drained ground pork
- 1/2 lb Shelled shrimp (save the-shells!)
- 3 Firm fried tofu cut-into cubes
- 1 lg Sliced onion
- 3 Cloves crushed garlic

- 1 lb Turnips cut into strips
- 1 lb Potatoes cut into cubes
- 2 lb Pole beans cleaned and cut-crosswise
- 1 bunch Lettuce (not iceberg)
- 2 Tsp Soy sauce
- 4 Tsp Vegetable oil
- 1tsp   Salt and pepper
- 2 Tsp Fish sauce (patis) optional
- 2 Tsp Accent salt optional
- 1 pkg Lumpia wrappers

Preparation

- For the stock, boil the shrimp shells in 1 1/2 cups water. Sauté the garlic, onions, ground port, shrimp, and tofu. Add the potatoes and 1/2 cup stock.
- Cook for 10 minutes, stirring constantly. Add the beans and cook for another 5 - 10 minutes. Then add turnips, soy sauce, vegetable oil, salt and pepper (to taste), and fish sauce.
- Continue to stir and cook for 5 more minutes. Drain and save the broth for the dipping sauce. Allow the mixture to cool. Separate the lumpier wrappers carefully.
- Line one end of the wrapper with a small piece of lettuce so that the lettuce pokes out a little bit - this is the top of the roll.
- Use 2 tbsp. of the mixture for filling (this will be a fatter roll than for fried lumpier) on top of the lettuce and roll the wrapper.
- Close the bottom end of the roll by folding it and securing it with a little water. Wrap each roll with wax paper.
- Makes 2 dozen, depending on size of roll. Spread garlic sauce (below) liberally over lumpia.

Fried Lumpia

Ingredients

- 1/4 cup Cider vinegar
- 1 tsp Soy sauce
- 1/2 cup Sugar
- 1 Cup Water (or pineapple juice)
- 1/2 tsp Finely grated gingerroot
- 1/2 C rushed garlic clove
- 2 Tsp Blended cornstarch with
- 2 Tsp Cold water
- 1 Salt

- 1/2 lb ground pork
- 1/2 lb finely chopped uncooked shrimp
- 1/2 cup minced mushrooms
- 1/2 cup Dices and peeled jicama
- 2   Finely chopped green onions
- 3   Egg yolks
- 2 Tsp Soy sauce
- 1 Lumpia wrappers
- 1 Oil for deep-frying

Preparation

- To make sauce, combine vinegar, 1 teaspoon soy sauce, sugar, water, ginger and garlic in small saucepan. Bring to boil.
- Stir in cornstarch paste and simmer 5 minutes, or until thickened. Season to taste with salt. Keep warm. For lumpia, mix pork, shrimp, mushrooms, jicama, green onions, egg yolks and 2 tablespoons soy sauce in bowl.
- Mix well. Shape about 1 ½ tablespoons meat mixture into strip and place along one side of lumpia wrapper. Roll tightly, folding in wrapper ends while rolling. Moisten edges lightly with water to seal.
- Repeat with remaining filling. Fry in deep hot oil until golden brown. Serve whole or cut in halves or thirds. Serve with sweet-sour sauce.

Hot and Sour Shrimp
With Watercress and Walnut

Ingredients

- 1 lb Butter shrimp deveined large uncooked-peeled
- 4 Tsp Dry sherry
- 1 Tsp Grated fresh ginger peeled
- 1/2 cup Chicken stock (or)Canned-broth
- 2 Tsp Soy sauce
- 2 Tsp Catsup. 1 Tsp Cornstarch
- 1 Tsp Rice vinegar (or white wine) –vinegar
- 1 Tsp Sugar
- 1 tsp Oriental sesame oil
- 1/4 tsp Cayenne pepper
- 6 Tsp Peanut oil
- 2 Tsp Chopped walnuts
- 3 Bunch trimmed watercress
- 2 Med Cut into -1-inch squares bell peppers
- 2   Minced garlic cloves

- 8 Cut diagonally into 1-inch-long pieces green onions

Preparation
- Combine shrimp, 2 tablespoons Sherry and grated ginger in large bowl. Cover and refrigerate for 30 minutes.
- Mix remaining 2 tablespoons Sherry, chicken stock, soy sauce, catsup, cornstarch, rice vinegar, sugar, sesame oil and cayenne pepper in small bowl.
- Heat 2 teaspoons peanut oil in wok or heavy large skillet over high heat. Add walnuts and stir-fry for 1 minute. Transfer walnuts to plate using slotted spoon.
- Add watercress to wok and stir-fry until just wilted, about 1 minute. Divide watercress among plates. Add 2 teaspoons peanut oil, bell peppers and garlic to wok and stir-fry for 1 minute.
- Add remaining 2 teaspoons peanut oil, shrimp mixture and onions and stir- fry for 1 minute. Stir stock mixture,
- Add to wok and cook sauce until clear and thick, stirring frequently, 2 minutes. Spoon sauce and shrimp over watercress. Sprinkle with walnuts and serve.

Inihaw Na Bangus
(Grilled Milkfish)

Ingredients
- 1 Whole bangus (about 2 lbs) -or dressed white fish
- 2 slices lemon
- 1 1/2 tsp Salt
- 1/8 tsp Pepper
- 1/2 cup Chopped tomatoes
- 1/4 cup Chopped onions
- 2 Chopped green onions

Preparation
- With sharp knife, cut along back of the fish and remove the backbone Rub fish inside and out with lemon slices, sprinkle with salt and pepper
- Mix tomatoes, onions and green onions. Stuff fish with the mixture through its back opening. Wrap in foil and grill over live coals until done. (About 15 minutes on each side).
- Serve with lemon wedges or with a lemon juice and patis (fish sauce dip.

Filipino Ox-Tail Stew

Ingredients

- 1 String beans
- 1 Chunky butter peanut
- 1 Egg plant
- 1 Ox tail (of course)
- 1 Orr brand achuote

Preparation

- Boil (cook) the ox tail the night before until it is quite tender, but the meat doesn't fall off the bone. Remove the meat and cool the soup in the refrigerator.
- The next evening (or morning). Remove the fat. Cook the meat again and add egg plant, string beans and cook some more. Add the peanut butter.
- Mix the Achuote in water and add to the pot (only the liquid portion, strain the seeds) Let it cook some more. Fry some Bagoong (Shrimp paste) Serve with rice.

Lechon

Ingredients

- 1 S alt to taste
- 1 Lettuce leave for Garnish
- 1 h Lechon sauce
- 1 can liver pate (4 oz)
- 1 sm Finely chopped onion
- 1 tbs Vegetable oil
- 1 cup Water
- 3 tbs Vinegar
- 3 tbs Sugar
- 1/2 cup Bread crumbs
- 1 Salt and pepper to taste

Preparation

- Salt pork lightly. Place pork on a rack in a pan. Roast in a preheated oven at 350F. Allow 25 to 30 minutes cooking time for each pound of pork. In the meantime, prepare the lechon sauce.
- In a small pan over medium heat, sauté onion in oil until cooked. Add liver pate, water, vinegar, sugar, bread crumbs and salt and pepper to taste.
- Stir and let simmer for 8-10 minutes or until sauce has thickened. Correct seasonings. Set aside.
- Cut roast pork into small serving pieces and arrange on a platter with

lettuce leaves as garnish. Sere with the lechon sauce. Yield. 4-6 servings.

Manila Clams
With Black Bean and Ginger Sauce

Ingredients
- 2 tsp Peanut oil
- 2 Tsp Finely minced ginger
- 1 Tsp Finely minced garlic
- 1/4 cup Minced scallions
- 2 Dozen
- 1/4 cup Shao hosing (or dry sherry)
- 1 Tsp Oyster sauce
- 1 tsp Thin soy sauce
- 1/2 tsp Sugar
- 2 Tsp Salted black beans
- 2 tsp Cornstarch
- 1/2 tsp Sesame oil
- 1 Manila clams (or New -Zealand)
- 1 Cockles
- 1 Clever

Preparation

- Place oil in a wok over medium high heat. Stir fry the ginger, garlic, jalapeno, and scallions for 1 minute. Add the clams and stir well to blend.
- Add the Shoa Hsing and a scant 3/4 cup water. Cover wok, and boil the clams open for about 2 to 3 minutes. Remove clams and place in a colander; shake over wok to let the juices run off into wok.
- Set aside. To the wok, add the oyster sauce, the soy sauce, the sugar and the black beans. Stir well. Cook over medium high heat for 3 seconds.
- Mix the cornstarch in a small cup with a little water until a milky liquid is formed, and then add to the boiling liquid in the wok (which will thicken immediately).
- Stir well for 10 seconds, remove from heat, and add sesame oil. Return clams to wok and toss to coat. Serve immediately. 4 servings as a first course

Menudong Goto

Ingredients
- 500 gms Tripe (goto)
- 2 Tsp Cooking oil
- 2 cloves crushed garlic
- 1 Chopped onion
- 1 Sliced chorizo de bilbao (Spanish 1 sausage)
- 1 Cup tomato sauce
- 1 Red (or green pepper)
- 1 cup Cooked garbanzos (chick peas)
- 2 cup Broth
- 2 Fried and cubed potatoes
- 1 To taste salt
- 1 tsp Vetsin (msg)

Preparation
- Clean and boil tripe in salt and water until tender. Cut into small pieces and set aside. Fry the garlic and onions in hot oil. Add the chorizo de bilbao and pour in tomato sauce.
- Drop in tripe, pepper, garbanzos and potatoes. Simmer until sauce is of desired consistency. Just before removing from the fire, season with salt and Vetsin

Monggo

Ingredients
- 1 cup whole monggo (mung) beans
- 5 Tsp Vegetable oil
- 7 Light garlic cloves
- 1 Mashed 2 medium-sized onions
- 3/4 lb Chopped red-ripe tomatoes
- 1/2 lb malunggay leaves (substitute1 spinach (or kangkong))
- 1 tsp Salt

Preparation
- In a casserole, put water, munggo, and Knorr pork cube
- Bring to a boil and simmer for 30 minutes or until the munggo is cooked
- In a skillet, heat the oil and saute the garlic, onion, and tomatoes.
- Add the pork and saute until lightly browned.
- Add in the munggo and stock.
- Season with pepper and add the malunggay leaves.

Monkey Meat

Ingredients
- 2 lb. pork steaks (or actual monkey meat is eaten in the Philippines)
- ½ cup teriyaki marinade
- ¼ cup chicken broth
- 1 TB minced garlic
- ½ TB crushed ginger
- Pepper
- 12 bamboo skewers (soaked in water)

Preparation
- Cut up pork steaks (or monkey meat) into bite size pieces.
- Mix the teriyaki, broth, garlic, ginger and pepper together. Place the meat in a container and pour the marinade over it.
- Place an air tight lid on the container and
- Marinade over night.
- Place on presoaked bamboo skewers and grill on a foil covered grill that has been sprayed with cooking spray. Grill until dark brown. 20 minutes is a guess, it really depends on the cut and temp of the grill.
- Great served with rice

Alternate Preparation
- Marinate sliced pork in 7-up. That's right, 7-up. If you want, you can add a little garlic and/or onion to the marinade. The pork is then skewered and grilled, basting with soy sauce while cooking.
- It sounds bizarre, but the 7-up would give a citrusy taste like lemon juice.

Pickled Pork Snouts
(Kilawin)

Ingredients

- 1 lb Pork snout (or 1 pkg)
- 1/2 cup Palm vinegar
- 1/4 cup Soy sauce
- 1/2 tsp pepper corns or, Cracked -ground black pepper
- 1 med Chopped onion (or green)
- 4 Minced garlic clove
- 2 Fresh sliced jalapenos
- 1 Pkg fried tufu
- 1 Shredded green papaya-(optional)

Preparation

- Procedure: Clean hairs from pork snouts by scrapping them with a knife. Remove excess fat. When snouts are clean put them in a pot and cover with enough water to boil.
- When you think that the snouts are tender and soft let them cool off and then cut the snouts into inch size pieces.
- Mix the rest of the ingredients in with the cut snouts. Taste a little bit so you can see if you need to add more of one or two of the ingredients to suit your taste.

###

Part 13: Russian Recipes

Russian cuisine *derives its rich and varied character from the vast and multi-cultural expanse of Russia. Its foundations were laid by the peasant food of the rural population in an often harsh climate, with a combination of plentiful fish, poultry, game, mushrooms, berries, and honey.*

Crops of grains provided a plethora of breads, beers and vodka. Flavorful soups and stews are centered on seasonal or storable produce, fish, and meats. This wholly native food remained the staple for the vast majority of Russians well into the 20th century.

Russian Kulich

Ingredients

- 1/2 tsp Saffron
- 1/2 cup Sliced glazed fruits Sliced (cherries, pineapple, citrus)
- 1/2 cup Raisins
- 3 pkg Dry yeast
- 2 Tsp Light brown sugar
- 1/4 cup dark rum
- 1 cup Almonds (toasted & Sliced-coarsely, chopped)
- 1 cup Sifted flour
- 1/4 cup Scalded & cooled milk
- 3/4 cup Unsalted-butter
- 1 cup light brown sugar
- 1 tsp Anise extract
- 1 tsp Almond extract
- 3 Egg yolks
- 1 cup Whipping cream, half & half-or table cream
- 4 5 cup Flour
- 3 Egg white
- 1 Stiffly beaten egg white
- 2 cup Powdered sugar
- 1 tsp Vanilla (or almond extract)

Preparation

- Soak saffron in rum an hour or more. Combine fruits, raisins and almonds with 1 cup flour. Set aside Dissolve yeast with milk and 2 tablespoons sugar.
- Allow to stand 5-10 minutes. In electric mixer, cream butter and sugar until smooth. Add extracts, Add 4 cups flour and beat until smooth and elastic, adding additional flour as necessary.
- Place in oiled bowl, turning to coat top of dough. Cover with plastic wrap and a towel wrung out in cold water. Allow to rise in warm place until doubled. Punch down dough.
- Turn out onto lightly floured board and knead in floured fruits and nuts, saffron and rum. If dough becomes sticky. Add flour, 1/4 cup at a time.
- Beat egg whites until stiff. Fold into dough with metal scraper or spatula. Sprinkle with a bit more flour. Thoroughly oil 2 (2 pound) coffee cans.
- Cut and oil waxed paper circles to fit bottom of cans. Fill each can halfway with dough. Moisten fingers and pat tops smooth.

- Cover with waxed paper and allow rising in warm place until double reaches no higher than top edge of cans.
- Bake at 375 degrees for 20 minutes. Turn down heat to 325 degrees and bake 40 minutes. Cool 10 minutes. Turn out of can by using long thin knife to loosen. Frost while still warm.

Bliny

Ingredients
- 2 Servings
- 3/4 cups Flour
- 1 tsp Granulated sugar
- 1 tsp Shortening
- 1 1/2 tsp Yeast
- 1/2 tsp Salt
- 1 Separated egg
- 1 1/2 cups Milk
- 2 tsp vegetable oil

Preparation
- Heat 3/4 of milk to 35C (about 95F). Add yeast till fully dissolved. Add half of sugar, yolk, melted shortening - keep stirring. Add half of flour. Stir batter until smooth.
- Cover with cloth and let stand for 1-1/2 to 2 hours. It should rise to double its original size. Mix, heat remaining milk to 50C (this would be about 120F, I think –
- I'm just converting the Laakso temperatures in my head, and my Fahrenheit is a bit shaky), pour in. Fold in remaining four, sugar, and gradually, well-beaten egg-white.
- Cover with cloth and leave for 2-1/2 to 3-1/2 hours. Brush large skillet with the vegetable oil. Heat until quite hot. Spoon batter onto skillet to cover the surface.
- Turn blin over when one side is a nice golden color. Serve hot. Serves two.

Borsch

Ingredients
- 1 cup Dry navy beans
- 2 1/2 lb Lean Beef
- 1/2 lb Slab bacon
- 10 cups Cold water

- 1 Bay leaf
- 8 Whole peppercorns
- 2 Garlic cloves
- 2 Tsp Dried parsley
- 1 Carrot
- 1 Celery stalk
- 1 lg Red onion
- 1 tsp Salt (opt)
- 8 Beets for soup
- 2 sm Beets
- 2 cups Green Shredded cabbage
- 2 lg Sliced leeks
- 3 med Cut potatoes into eighths
- 1 can (1 lb 13 oz) Tomatoes
- 1 Tsp Tomato paste
- 3 Tsp Red wine vinegar
- 4 Tsp Sugar
- 1 lb Kielbasa (opt)
- 2 Tsp Flour
- 1 Tsp Melted butter
- 1/2 cup Sour cream (opt)

Preparation

- Cover beans with water and allow soaking overnight; cooking until tender; draining; setting aside. Place beef, bacon and water in large soup pot; bring to a boil.
- Skim fat from surface. Add bay leaf, peppercorns, garlic, parsley, carrot, celery, onion and salt. Cover and simmer over low heat for about 1 1/2 hours. Scrub beets for soup and cook in boiling water until tender, about 45 minutes; drain and discard water; cool.
- Peel and cut each beet into eighths. Scrub small beets; grate; cover with water to soak.
- Remove meat from soup; set aside. Strain soup into another pot and add cooked beets, cabbage, leeks, potatoes, tomatoes, tomato paste, vinegar, sugar, beef and bacon.
- Bring to a boil and simmer 45 minutes. Cut kielbasa into chunks and add with navy beans to soup. Simmer 20 minutes more.
- Mix flour and butter together to form paste
- Stir into soup to thicken slightly. Strain raw beets, saving liquid and discarding beets. Add beet liquid to soup. Additional sugar or vinegar may be added for sweeter or sourer flavor.
- Slice meat and arrange in individual soup bowls. Pour hot soup with vegetables over meat. Garnish each serving with a dollop of sour cream, if

desired.

Caviar Patrijani
(Georgian Caviar)

Ingredients
- 4 cups Water
- 2 lg (1-1/2 lbs) Eggplants
- 2 med (1 cup) ripe tomatoes –quartered
- 2 (1 cup) cored and seeded red (or green sweet) pepper
- 2 Tsp corn oil
- 2 med (1 cup)Chopped onions
- 2 Finely chopped garlic cloves
- 1 tsp salt
- 1/4 tsp pepper
- 1 tsp red-wine vinegar

Preparation
- Bring 4 c water to a boil in large pan, put in whole eggplants, cover, & cook over moderate heat for 15 mins, which is enough to soften them.
- Drain, cool, & peel eggplants. Press the liquid gently thru metal sieve. Process tomatoes & peppers to a puree, then add eggplant.
- Heat oil in a skillet & stir-fry onions over moderate heat for 2 to 3 mins, until golden. Add puree & stir-fry over low heat for 10 mins.
- Turn out mixture into bowl & briskly stir in garlic, salt, pepper, & wine vinegar. Refrigerate. Serve cold or at room temp. Makes 4-6 servings.

Circassian Chicken

Ingredients
- 3 1/2 lb Stewing chicken
- 1 sm Scrapped & diced carrot
- 1 med Peeled and Chopped onion
- 1/4 cup Fresh parsley
- 1 Salt -To Taste
- 1 Pepper --To Taste
- 2 cups Shelled walnuts
- 3 Stale white bread Slices

- 1 lg Peeled and Chopped onion
- 1 Tsp Paprika

Preparation

- Put chicken, carrot, onion, parsley, salt, pepper and 5 cups of water in a large kettle. Bring to a boil. Reduce heat and simmer, covered, for 2 hours, or until tender.
- The exact simmering time will depend on the age of the chicken. Remove chicken from kettle to cool. Strain broth and reserve.
- Cut meat into shreds. Out the walnuts through a meat grinder twice. After each grinding reserve the oil separately from the nuts.
- Soak bread in some of the strained chicken broth until soft. Squeeze dry and mix with ground walnuts, onion and pepper.
- Put this mixture through a meat grinder 2 more times. Then gradually add about 1 cup of the strained chicken broth to the mixture to make a paste or sort of mayonnaise-type sauce.
- Combine 1/2 of this sauce with the shredded chicken and spread evenly on a platter.
- Cover with remaining sauce. Garnish with the reserved walnut oil by sprinkling it, along with the paprika, over the sauce.

Deruny
(Ukrainian Potato Pancakes)

Ingredients

- 1 lg Grated onion
- 6 Peeled & grated potatoes
- 2 Tsp Flour
- 2 Eggs
- 2 tsp salt
- 3/4 tsp Black pepper
- 1 pt Sour cream
- 1/2 pt Cream

Preparation

- In a large bowl use a mixer to puree the ingredients except the sour cream & cream. You may do this in a food processor as well or a blender.
- Heat oil in a skillet and when hot drop large spoons full of the mixture. Cook until browned on one side. Turn and repeat. When done remove, drain, and place in a warm oven.
- Mix the sour cream & cream together. Serve warm with a large dollop of the cream mixture! This a staple in Ukrainian homes and these pancakes

- will store well in the refrigerator for 2-3 days.
- In many homes preserves or jam is also served on these delicious pancakes.

Georgian Cheese Pastries

Ingredients

- 1 ½ All purpose cup flour
- 1/2 tsp Salt
- 1/2 tsp Tartar cream
- 10 Tsp Cold and unsalted butter
- 1/4 cup Ice water
- 1 Egg
- 1 cup Shredded muenster cheese
- 1 cup Shredded cheddar cheese,
- 3 Tsp Grated parmesan cheese
- 1/4 cup Chopped parsley
- 2 Tsp Chopped chives,
- 2 Tsp Chopped mint

Preparation

- Prepare Pastry: Place flour, salt, cream of tartar and butter in food processor. Whirl until texture of coarse meal. Add water.
- Whirl just until combined and mixture begins to mass together. Place on plastic wrap, flatten to a disk, and wrap airtight.
- Refrigerate at least 1 hour or up to 30 days. Roll dough on floured surface to 1/8" thickness. Cut out 24 circles with 3" round cookie cutter,
- Re-rolling scraps; or trace around 3" water glass. Pleat edges of circles and fit in bottom of muffin tins.
- Prepare Filling: Beat egg in bowl. Add Muenster, Cheddar, Parmesan, parsley, chives and mint.
- Spoon 2 teaspoons filling in each pastry shell; spread level. (Can be prepared up to 3 hours ahead and refrigerated.)

Georgian Chicken

Ingredients

- 1 Whole roasting chicken
- 1 Pounds
- 1 lLmon
- 3 Tsp Oil
- 3 Chopped onions,
- 2 cups Ground beef (or lamb)
- 1/2 tsp pepper
- 1/2 tsp Ground cinnamon
- 1/4 tsp Ground nutmeg
- 1/4 tsp Ground cloves
- 1/2 tsp Salt
- 2 cups Unsweetened red grape juice
- 1 tsp Sugar
- 1/2 cup Water
- 2 Tsp Halved blanched almonds
- 1 Garnished grapes

Preparation

- Squeeze juice from lemon and reserve. Rub the empty lemon halves over chicken.
- Sauté onions in hot oil, until transparent. Add beef or lamb and sauté, stirring, until meat is just cooked [redness gone]. Drain excess fat and reserve.
- Sauté meat another 5 minutes. Add spices, salt, 1 cup grape juice, lemon juice and sugar. Cook, constantly stirring, until most of the liquid has evaporated.
- Stuff the chicken with the meat mixture. Pour saved fat into skillet and brown chicken on all sides. Transfer browned, stuffed chicken to dutch oven, add 1/2 C grape juice, water and almonds.
- Cover tightly and simmer over low heat for approximately 3 hours, or until chicken is thoroughly cooked.

Georgian Potato Soup

Ingredients

- 6 cups Diced potatoes
- 1/2 cup small chopped onions
- 1/4 cup Chopped scallions
- 1 cup Apple sauce
- 1/4 cup Apple juice

- 3 cups Chicken stock or-
- 3 cups Vegetable stock
- 1 1/4 cups   heavy cream
- 1/2 Cup Cottage cheese
- 1/3 cup Raisins
- 1 Minced garlic clove
- 1/3 cup Chopped dried apricots
- 2 1/2 Tsp flour

Preparation
- Mix 1 cup of the cream, the cottage cheese, & the flour in mixing bowl. Beat until smooth then blend in the remaining cream.
- This can be done by hand, with a hand mixer, or in a blender. Set aside in refrigerator. Mix all of the spices together and divide into 2 equal portions.
- Take a large, heavy pot and place on HIGH heat for 3-4 minutes. Add the vegetables except for 2 cups of the diced potatoes. And 1 of the spice portions.
- Stir and cook over the High heat for 4-6 minutes being sure to scrape the crusts that form on the bottom of the pot. Add the apple juice and then the apple sauce.
- Stir & cook for 2-3 minutes then add the stock, the other spice portion. Cook while stirring for 12 minutes. Remove and either rice the mixture or puree it in a blender until it is smooth.
- Return to the pot, add the 2 cups of diced potatoes, bring to a boil, reduce heat to Low, stir well, cover and cook for 15 minutes. Add more stock if more liquid is need.
- Blend in the cream mixture and continue to cook stirring as you do for 3-4 minutes.

Green Borscht

Ingredients
- 7 1/2 cups Beef stock
- 1 1/2 lb Spinach
- 2 Carrots
- 1/2 Small turnip
- 1 Medium potato
- 1 Onion
- 2 Celery sticks
- 1 Salt and pepper

- 1/2 Lemon juice
- 1 tsp Sugar
- 3 Hard Boiled eggs
- 6 Tsp Sour cream

Preparation

- Remove the hard stems from the spinach and wash it thoroughly. Put it in a saucepan with a little salted water. Cover and boil for 15 minutes or until cooked.
- Sieve and transfer it to stock together with the water it has been cooked in. Peel and wash the rest of the vegetables and cut them into fine strips. Add them to the stock
- Bring to the boil and season. Cover and simmer for about 20 minutes. Add the lemon juice and a little sugar and serve with one dessert spoon of sour cream and a little chopped hard boiled eggs to each plate.
- This is best when the spinach is young in the spring. Serve with rye bread. Frozen spinach does work also.

Hearty Russian Beet Soup Hot

Ingredients

- 1 cup Dry navy beans
- 2 1/2 lb Lean beef
- 1/2 lb Slab bacon
- 10 cups Cold water
- 1 Bay leaf
- 8 Whole peppercorns
- 2 Garlic cloves
- 2 Tsp Dried parsley
- 1 Carrot
- 1 Celery stalk
- 1 Large red onion
- 1 tsp Salt (opt)
- 8 Beets for soup
- 2 Small beets
- 2 cups Shredded green cabbage
- 2 Large Sliced leeks
- 3 Medium cut potatoes
- 1 into eighths
- 1 can (1 lb 13 oz) Tomatoes

- 1 Tsp Tomato paste
- 3 Tsp Red wine vinegar
- 4 Tsp Sugar
- 1 lb Kielbasa (opt)
- 2sp Tsp flour
- 1 Tsp Melted butter
- 1/2 cup Sour cream (opt)

Preparation

- Cover beans with water and allow soaking overnight; cooking until tender; draining; setting aside. Place beef, bacon and water in large soup pot; bring to a boil.
- Skim fat from surface. Add bay leaf, peppercorns, garlic, parsley, carrot, celery, onion and salt. Cover and simmer over low heat for about 1 1/2 hours.
- Scrub beets for soup and cook in boiling water until tender, about 45 minutes; drain and discard water; cool. Peel and cut each beet into eighths. Scrub small beets; grate; cover with water to soak.

Homemade Sausage With Onions

Ingredients

- 2 lb Pork
- 1 lb Fat salt pork
- 8 cups Garlic
- 8 peppercorns
- 3 tsp Salt

Preparation

- Run the all the pork and 1/2 pound of the salt pork through the coarse plate of a mincer. Run the remaining 1/2 pound salt pork through the fine plate of the mincer.
- Mix the two ground meat mixtures together. Grind the garlic and add to the mixture, along with the peppercorns (coarsely cracked) and the salt.
- Stuff the sausage skins and refrigerate for 5 to 6 hours. Prick sausage skin in several spots with a fork and sauté in a little fat with onion.
- For prolonged storage, put sausage into enameled or ceramic dish and cover with melted lard.

Kugelis Potato Pudding

Ingredients
- 6 oz Thick cut bacon
- 1 1/8 inch pieces
- 6 lb Peeled russet potatoes
- 1 Finely Grated
- 1 Medium and peeled yellow onion
- 1 Grated finely
- 5 oz can Milk evaporated
- 5 Beaten eggs
- 2 tsp Salt
- 1 Freshly ground black pepper to taste
- 1 Tsp Melted butter

Preparation
- Run the grated potato and onion through a meat grinder on coarse. Place in a mixing bowl. Add the bacon with its drippings and remaining ingredients except the butter.
- Use the melted butter to butter the baking dish. Mix well and pour into a 13 x 8 x 2 inch glass baking dish. Bake at 425 for 1/2 hour, then reduce the heat to 375 for 25 minutes more.
- NOTE: for best results the pudding should be at least TWO inches deep in the pan.

Kulich

Ingredients
- 1/3 cup Golden raisins
- 3 Tsp Rum
- 1/2 cup Sugar
- 1 pkg Active dry yeast (1/4 oz)
- 1/2 cup Water
- Warm (105-115')
- 6 T sp Butter and softened (3/4 stick)
- 3 Eggs
- 2 Tsp Vanilla
- 3 Tsp Milk powdered

- 3/4 tsp Salt
- 1/8 tsp ground saffron (optional)
- 4 3/4 cup All-purpose flour
- 1/4 cup Slivered almonds
- 1/4 cup Chopped and candied orange peel
- SUGAR GLAZE
- 1 cup Confectioners' sugar
- 1 Reserved soaking rum
- 2 tsp Lemon juice
- 1 tsp Water

Preparation

- Soak raisins in rum for at least 30 or overnight. Combine 1/2 teaspoon sugar along with yeast and water in small bowl. Let stand until foamy, about 5 minutes.
- Beat together remaining sugar, butter, eggs, vanilla, powdered milk, salt and saffron, if using, and yeast mixture in large bowl with mixer until blended.
- Add 2 cups of the flour and 1 tablespoon of soaking rum, beating for 2 minutes at high speed.
- Drain raisins and reserve rum for glaze. Stir raisins, almonds and orange peel into dough with wooden spoon. Stir in enough of remaining flour to form soft dough.
- Turn out onto floured surface and knead until smooth and elastic, about 5 minutes. Place dough in greased bowl, turning to coat. Cover; let rise in warm spot for 1 1/2-2 hours, until doubled.
- Grease well two 1 lb. coffee cans. Line bottoms with rounds of waxed paper. Turn dough out onto floured surface. Punch down; knead a few turns. Divide in half and place in prepared cans. (They should be about two-thirds full.)
- Let rise, covered, for about 1 1/2 hours, or until it has risen to top of can. Preheat oven to moderate (350'F). Brush tops of breads lightly with water.
- Bake in lower third of preheated moderate over (350'F) for 35-40 minutes or until golden brown on top and long skewer inserted in center comes out clean.
- Check after 25 minutes and tent foil if browning too quickly. Using oven mitts, carefully remove the bread from the cans, supporting top of bread and twisting off can.
- Cool upright on wire rack to room temperature. Drizzle glaze over breads. Garnish with candied orange peel and slivered almonds, if you wish.
- SUGAR GLAZE: Stir together confectioners' sugar, reserved soaking rum, lemon juice and water as need, in small bowl until good drizzling consistency.

Mocha Honey Cream Torte

Ingredients

- 6 Large eggs
- 6 cups Mocha custard cream <see below>
- 2 tsp Baking soda
- 1/2 cup Sunflower oil
- 1 1/3 cup Sugar
- 1 1/3 cup Honey
- 3 1/2 cup Flour
- 1 tsp Baking powder
- 1 cup Strong coffee
- 1 cup Apricot preserves (or jams)
- 1/2 cup Sweet sherry
- 1 Fine dry bread crumbs
- 1 Butter
- MOCHA CUSTARD CREAM
- 12 oz Evaporated milk
- 1 Vanilla pudding package not instant
- 2 Egg yolks
- 4 oz Unsalted butter
- 1/2 cup Sugar powdered
- 1/2 cup Strong coffee
- 2 Tsp Instant coffee
- 1/2 cup Sweet sherry

Preparation

- Mocha Cream Custard directions: Slowly add the evaporated milk in a large sauce pan. To the pudding mix Save 2 tablespoons for use later in the recipe.
- Stir constantly and cook over medium heat. Beat the egg yolks with the 2 tablespoons of milk until they are frothy, add to the mixture, and bring to a boil for 5 minutes being sure to keep the boil very slight.
- Heat the coffee, mix in the instant coffee and add to the pudding stirring well. Set this aside, covers, and cool. Cream the butter & sugar in a large bowl until fluffy.
- Scrape the sides of the bowl and add 3-4 tablespoons of the pudding, mix well, add the remaining pudding in 2 parts, and beat after each addition of pudding.
- This may be refrigerated for 2-3 days but be sure to bring to room temp

before using. Torte directions: Butter 2 springs form pans <9"> be sure to cover the sides.
- Sprinkle the bread crumbs even to the rim. Shake out the excess. Separate the eggs. Beat the yolks with sugar until they are fluffy, add oil and beat until pale, add honey and beat again.
- Combine dry ingredients and sift, add to yolk mixture in 1/3's, while stirring add the coffee. Whip the egg whites until they become stiff and fold into the mixture.
- Pour into the spring form pans and bake in a pre-heated oven at 350 degrees F for 1 hour. Cool slightly, remove form pan, and place on cooling racks. Cut torte into 3 layers.
- Place 1 layer on 2 crossed pieces of wax paper, sprinkle with a little of the sherry, and spread with a thin coating of the apricot jam, then with the mocha cream, add the next layer and repeat, then cover with the remaining layer.
- Sprinkle with sherry, cover with foil, and refrigerate for 6 hours. Ice with the remaining mocha cream. You may or may not wish to decorate the top.

Pirohy
(Porusynykovi)

Ingredients
- 4 cups Flour
- 1 Beaten egg slightly
- 1/2 tsp Salt
- 2 cups warm potato water
- 1 Plain water
- 1 Potato filling
- 3 lb Pared potatoes cut into 1 small pieces.
- Boiled mashed
- 1/3 lb Grated yellow cheese
- 1 (American, Colby or similar 1 mild cheese)
- 1 Cheese filling
- 1/2 lb Dry mashed cottage cheese (to eliminate the lumps)
- Salt/herb version
- 1/2 tsp Salt
- 1 Chopped scant tablespoon
- 1 Green dill weed (or chives.)
- 1 Sweet version
- 1 Sugar to taste

- 1 Cinnamon to taste
- 1/4 cup White raisins
- 1 Cabbage filling
- 1 Medium chopped onion
- 2 tsp margarine
- 1 Medium head cabbage
- 1 qt Sauerkraut juice
- 14 oz can of Sauerkraut, do not rinse

Preparation

- Chop raw cabbage, combine with sauerkraut, including original juice, and simmer together for an hour. Add a little water if needed. After it is cooked, drain liquid.
- Sauté the onion in the margarine until it is clear. Add the drained cabbage, and fry slowly, stirring often until it loses the whitish look and is rather dry. Add salt and pepper to taste.
- Assembly
- Roll out dough on a floured board to about 1/8 inch thickness. Cut 2 or 3 inch circles. It is a rather sticky dough but this makes it seal very well.
- Place about a teaspoon of filling to one side of the circle, lap over the other half so it is like a half moon and seal the edges by punching together carefully.
- Cooking
- Have an 8 to 10 quart pot of water at a rolling boil. Drop 6 pirohy into the water one by one. Stir with a wooden spoon. Water must be kept boiling at all times.
- When they rise to the top of the water, continue cooking for another minute. Remove with a slotted spoon and place into a colander.
- While the next 6 are cooking, coat the first 6 with butter or oleo by placing them into a skillet containing melted butter.
- Remove and place them into a roaster or other container, for serving or reheating at a later time. This method works well when large quantities are being made.

Piroshki

Ingredients

- 1 lb Ground beef
- 4 1/2 cups Bisquick
- 1 1/3 cups Milk
- 1 lb Ground beef

- 1 lb Ground chicken
- 1 tsp Oregano
- 1 Tsp Garlic powder
- 1 Tsp Black pepper
- 1/2 tsp Sage
- 1/2 tsp Thyme
- 16 oz Creamed corn
- 1 pkg Lipton vegetable soup mix

Preparation

- Heat oven to 350 F. In a bowl, mix the pepper, garlic powder, oregano and thyme together with the ground beef and ground chicken. Sauté the meat mixture until brown; drain well.
- Set aside. Combine the creamed corn and the envelope of soup mix in a saucepan; mix thoroughly and heat until warmed through.
- Add the meat mixture; mix together well. The mixture should be moist but not soupy. Make the dough from the Bisquick and milk; roll out medium-thin on a board well-dusted with more Bisquick.
- The dough will be fairly sticky, so have a fair amount of extra Bisquick on hand to dust the board and the pin again as needed. Cut out 4" diameter rounds (I find an English muffin ring or a large tuna can works well).
- Take a scant tablespoon of the filling and place off-center on each round; fold the other half over and pinch to seal. (Hint: when trying to loosen the rolled-out dough from the board, use a metal spatula.)
- The piroshki will tend to separate at the seam in the oven, so seal them pretty solidly. Place piroshki on a cookie sheet or jelly roll pan; brush with an egg wash to help it seal.
- Place in the oven and bake for 30 minutes. Remove from oven and cool a few minutes; serve warm.

Pisznyi Borscht

Ingredients
- 2 lb Beets
- 2 Carrots
- 1 Parsnip
- 1 Turnip
- 2 Large celery ribs
- 2 Chopped onions medium finely
- 1 lg Bay leaf
- 4 Peppercorns

- 1/2 lb Chopped mushrooms
- 1 qt beet kvas
- 2 tsp Salt
- 1 tsp Ground pepper
- 1 Tsp Chopped fresh dill

Preparation

- Scrub the beets and cut into quarters. Cover with water and cook over low heat until tender, about 1 to 2 hours. Cool and pour off the liquid, reserving it.
- Slip off the peels. (Wear rubber gloves to prevent purple hands.) This may be done a day in advance. Peel and cut up the other vegetables.
- Add the bay leaf, peppercorns, and boletus or mushrooms to the vegetables, with enough water to cover, and cook, in a large aluminum pot over low heat, until tender. Strain the beet liquid into the vegetables.
- Shred the beets in a processor or on a medium grater, and add. Simmer for about 10 minutes and strain into a large pot. To keep the broth clear, do not press the vegetables.
- Add the beet kvas, mushroom liquid, pepper and salt. Bring to a gentle boil, then turn the heat low. Taste, the flavor should be tart, mellow, and full. For more tartness, add fresh lemon juice or sour salt. Keeps well in the refrigerator.
- Reheat gently; do not over cook or the color will turn brown. To serve, pour over 3 or 4 varinyki in soup plates and garnish with the fresh dill a large dollop of sour cream.

Pork and Mushroom Stroganoff

Ingredients
- 3/4 lb Fettuccine
- 1 Tsp Oil
- 1 lb Pork schnitzel
- 1 Strip
- 1 Sliced onion
- 1 pkg Mushroom soup mix
- 1 cup Water
- 2 Tsp Tomato paste
- 6 oz Mushrooms
- 1/2 cup Reduced cream
- 2 Tsp Lemon juice

Preparation

- Cook pasta following packet directions. Prepare sauce while pasta is cooking. Heat oil in frying pan. Add pork & onion. Stir fry for 2-3 minutes. Combine soup mix, water & tomato paste.
- Add to pan with mushrooms. Bring to the boil, stirring, and then simmer for 5 minutes. Stir in reduced cream & lemon juice. Drain pasta; place on serving plates. Serve pork & mushroom mixture on top.

Romee
(Cornmeal Mush)

Ingredients

- 1 cup Instant cornmeal white (or yellow)
- 6 cups Cold water

Preparation

- When did corn travel from Valley of Mexico to Georgian? It had to have been after Spanish conquest in sixteenth century, along with tomatoes & peppers.
- In any event, Georgians incorporated it into their cooking & unseasoned mush is eaten with sharply seasoned meat dishes such as steamed (see GEORGIAN.023) Mix cornmeal & water together in a solid-weight metal pan and bring to a boil.
- Reduce heat to low & cook, uncovered, for 40 mins. Stir mixture now & then. When ready meal will have absorbed water & mush will be firm enough to slice, yet moist enough to have a smooth consistency.
- Serve hot while still in pan by scooping of slicing out serving portions.

Siberian Huskies
(Russian Dumplings with Cabbage)

Ingredients

- 1 1/2 Tsp Corn oil
- 8 cups Sliced very thinly cabbage
- 2 lg Sliced onions thinly
- 3/4 cup Chicken broth
- 2 tsp to 3-tsp Dijon mustard
- 3/4 tsp Worcestershire sauce

- 1/2 tsp Fennel seeds
- 1 Freshly Ground pepper to taste
- 1/2 tsp Salt (optional)
- 40 Cooked kalduni and drained (see master recipe)
- 2 tsp Chopped chives

Preparation

- The name of this dish came about when I saw the fat dumplings all mixed up in the cabbage.
- INSTRUCTIONS: Heat the oil in a large sauté pan over high heat. Add the cabbage and onions and sauté, tossing constantly, until the mixture is wilted, 4 to 5 minutes.
- Reduce heat to medium-low and continue to sauté, tossing occasionally, until the cabbage is very limp, almost velvety, about 20 minutes.
- Add the broth, mustard, Worcestershire and fennel; simmer for a minute. Add pepper and salt (if necessary).
- Add the kalduni and toss until cabbage and dumplings are thoroughly combined. Fold in the chives.

Siberian Pelmeni
(Meat-Filled Noodles)

Ingredients
- 3 cup Flour
- 1 tsp Salt
- 2 Egg yolks
- 2/3 cup Water
- 1 tbs Minus
- 1/2 lb Ground beef
- 1/2 lb Ground pork
- 2 Minced onions
- 2 Minced cloves garlic
- 1/4 lb Fresh chopped mushrooms fine optional
- 1 Pepper vinegar optional
- 1 Sour cream optional
- Brown butter optional
- 1 Spicy tomato sauce optional

Preparation
- Put flour in bowl. Press hollow in middle and add salt and egg yolks and

1/2 cup water. Using knife or big spoon, mix egg yolks first with water and then some of flour.
- Slowly add rest of water until mixture forms dough. Knead dough with both hands until workable and free of lumps. If dough is too sticky, add some flour.
- Dough should form solid ball. Sprinkle thin layer of flour onto flat surface. Divide dough into 3 pieces. Roll out 1 piece of dough until thin.
- Keep remaining dough covered under damp towel. Cut dough in circles about 2 inches in diameter. Repeat with remaining dough. Combine beef, pork, onions, garlic and mushrooms in bowl.
- Place 1 teaspoon meat mixture on each dough circle, then bend other side and press to seal, forming half-moons. Use some water, if necessary, brushed lightly on edges to make them stick.
- Keep finished pelmeni either on waxed paper or board sprinkled with flour. Pelmeni can be frozen at this point and cooked later.
- Cook 20 to 25 pelmeni at a time, uncovered, in plenty of rapidly boiling lightly salted water, about 5 minutes.
- Repeat until all pelmeni are cooked. Serve pelmeni either in clear soup (beef or, preferably, poultry) or as main course with pepper vinegar, sour cream, brown butter or spicy tomato sauce. Makes 60 pelmeni, or 4 main-course servings

Tushenaya Barinina
(Stewed Lamb/Mutton)

Ingredients
- 2 lb lamb (or mutton lean &) Boned
- 2 Tsp Vegetable oil
- 1 Tsp Tomato paste
- 1 cup Shredded cabbage
- 1 Sliced onion med
- 2 Sliced carrots
- 1 Salt to taste
- pepper to taste
- Minced garlic cloves
- 1/2 tsp Ground cinnamon
- Potatoes
- 1/2 Chopped cubes
- 1 cup Green peas
- 2 cup Beef broth
- 1 Sour cream

Preparation

- Cut meat into stew sized pieces and fry in the hot oil until browned along with the garlic and onion. Add the other ingredients and 1 cup of the beef broth.
- Simmer until done. Add more broth if necessary. Garnish with sour cream if you wish. Cooking Echo

Veal Stew With Cherries

Ingredients

- 2 lb Cubed veal boneless 1
- 4 Tsp Butter
- 2 Tsp Flour
- 1 cup Dried white beans
- 4 lg Chopped scallions whole
- 2 cups Canned sour cherries
- 1/2 cup Madeira (or port wine)
- 1 tsp Salt
- 1 Tsp White pepper
- 1 cup Cherry juice
- 1 tsp Ground freshly nutmeg
- 6 Tsp Sour cream

Preparation

- Soak beans overnight, rinse and cook until tender. Drain and set aside. Dredge veal in the flour then brown in butter.
- Add scallions, cherries, wine, cherry juice, salt & pepper, & the nutmeg to the veal. Bring to a boil, reduce the heat to low and simmer for 90 minutes.
- Add the beans to the pot approximately 20 minutes before serving. If possible make this stew a day in advance, refrigerate, then reheat. It tastes better that way. Add the sour cream as a garnish at serving.

Vryonoye Miaso Po-Russki
(Boiled Beef Russian)

Ingredients
- 1 lb Beef marrow bones
- 2 qt Water
- 1 cubed 1/2 Onion
- 1 Sliced carrot
- 2 celery Ribs w/leaves sliced
- 1 Peeled cubed 1/2 turnip
- 8 Whole peppercorns
- 2 Bay leaves
- 4 Tsp Fresh chopped parsley
- 4 Tsp Fresh chopped dill
- 3 lb Boneless beef rump roast
- 1 1/2 tsp Salt
- 2 Chopped garlic clove

Preparation
- Place the peppercorns, bay leaves, parsley, and dill into a small cloth bag. Tie the bag closed. Put water, marrow bones, the bag of spices, the vegetables, & salt into a large pot.
- Bring to a boil over high heat, skim the foam off as it occurs. Cook for 10 minutes at a boil, add the beef roast, boil for 3 minutes, reduce heat to low, cover, and simmer for 3 1/2 hours.
- Be sure to skim occasionally. Remove from heat, remove the roast from the pot, slice for serving.

Vushka
(Little Ear Dumplings)

Ingredients
- 2 cups unbleached all-purpose flour
- 1 tsp Salt
- 1 lg Egg yolk
- 1/2 cup evaporated milk
- 1/2 cup whole milk
- 1 tsp Oil (or melted butter)

Preparation

- Combine the flour and salt, blending well. Add the milk, egg yolk, and oil, again blending well. Allow to rest for 5 minutes.
- Knead for about minutes and form into a ball. (This may be done in a processor.) Cover and set aside for 15 minutes or so. On a floured surface, roll out a third of the dough, into a rectangle 1/8th inch thick.
- Turn the dough and roll from the center, so that all the dough in the rectangle is even in thickness. Run a hand under the dough to loosen it. Dust with flour and flip over and dust with flour.
- With a sharp knife, cut into 1 1/2-inch squares. Place a teaspoon of mushroom filling (see the next recipe in this series) in each square, being careful not to smear the edges.
- Fold on the diagonal to make a triangle. Pinch together the two bottom corners, wrapping it around your thumb with the point up (to resemble small ears on a cat), making sure that the edges have bonded or the stuffing will boil out.
- Place on cookie sheets covered with dish towels lightly dusted with flour. Repeat with the other pieces of dough, saving the scraps for last as the dough gets a little tougher when worked.
- Drop 10 or 12 vushka into 6 to 8 cups of rapidly boiling water and stir once with a wooden spoon, (The wooden spoon is very important as a metal one will lower the temperature of the water.) Do NOT cover.
- When they float to the top, cook 1 minute, then remove with a slotted spoon to a strainer. Cool on a lightly oiled plate without crowding.
- Repeat until all are cooked. Cover and set aside. These may be frozen and then reheated in boiling water. (DO NOT overcook when reheating.)

###

Part 14: USA Homestyle Recipes

America --The United States of America-- is truly a nation of immigrants—consisting of people from every region and country of the world. Therefore, it is not surprising that its cuisine is so diverse. Restaurant row sports foods of every persuasion: Italian, Chinese, French, German, Mexican, Polish, German, Japanese, Middle Eastern, and many other cuisines. However, the USA is also known for some of its favorite comfort foods. Americans, rich and not so rich, love hamburgers, hot dogs, meat loaf, barbeque, and other "comfort foods" which this section will emphasize.

Great American Steak Burger

Ingredients
- 2 lb. Fresh Ground Round or Ground Sirloin
- 2 garlic cloves or garlic powder
- Salt & Pepper if desired
- Cheese if desired (American, cheddar, soft cheddar, etc.,)
- 4 fresh onion rolls
- Any desired condiments, e.g., mustard, ketchup, mayo, onion, pickle, peppers

Preparation
- Chop garlic fine and mix thoroughly with meat
- Make four ½ pound patties from ground beef mixture
- Salt & pepper to taste
- Grill over hot charcoal until done the way you like it – rare to well done
- If desired, add cheese three-quarters through, let cheese melt
- Serve on a fresh bun (serves 4)

Kay's Onion Burgers

Ingredients
- 2 lb. Fresh Ground Round or Ground Sirloin
- 1 large package dried onion soup mix
- Salt & Pepper to taste
- Cheese if desired (American, cheddar, soft cheddar, etc.,)
- 4 fresh onion rolls
- Any desired condiments, e.g., mustard, ketchup, mayo, lettuce, tomato, onion slices, pickle slices, peppers

Preparation
- Thoroughly mix onion soup mix and meat
- Make four ½ pound patties from ground beef
- Grill over hot *charcoal* until done to taste
- If desired, add cheese three-quarters through, let cheese melt
- Salt & pepper to taste (note: onion soup mix contains a lot of sodium, may not need additional salt)
- Serve on a fresh bun (serves 4)

Famous Chicago Hot Dogs

Ingredients
- Premium beef hot dogs with casings
- Small, ripe tomato wedges
- Dill pickle spear
- Sport or other hot peppers
- Diced onions, marinated in milk
- Pickle relish
- Mustard & ketchup
- Fresh, steamed hot dog buns

Preparation
- Steam or charcoal desired number of dogs
- Put hot dogs on buns
- Add mustard and ketchup to taste
- Add pickle relish on top
- Add chopped onions on top
- Add tomato wedges and pickle spear on top
- Sprinkle celery salt on dog
- Last, add hot peppers, if desired

Detroit Super Bowl Coney Dogs

Ingredients
- Premium beef hot dogs with casings
- 1 can Hormel Chili (no beans)
- Chopped onions
- Mustard
- Cheese if desired
- Fresh, steamed hot dog buns

Preparation
- Heat chili
- Put desired number of hot dogs on buns
- Top with generous portion of chili
- Add cheese if desired
- Add mustard on top of chili

- Liberally top off with chopped onions
- Serves 4-8, depending on hot dog package

Mama's Old Fashioned Meatloaf

Ingredients
- 1 pound lean ground beef
- 1 pound ground pork
- 3/4 cup ketchup (reserve ¼ cup)
- 2 tbsp Worcestershire Sauce
- 1 cup chopped onions
- ½ cup chopped green pepper
- 1 cup bread crumbs
- 2 whole eggs
- 1 tsp garlic powder
- Salt & pepper to taste

Preparation
- Thoroughly mix all ingredients, preferably by hand
- When mixed, shape mixture into two loaves
- Spread remaining ketchup over top of loaves
- Put loaves in baking dish, add water to dish
- Bake at 350 degrees for 50-60 minutes, checking for doneness periodically (should not be pink on the inside)

Ron's Salmon Loaf

Ingredients
- 1- 16 oz. can of premium salmon without skin and larger bones
- 1 large onion, diced
- 2 eggs
- 2 cups bread crumbs
- 1 tsp garlic powder

Preparation
- Remove any left over skin from salmon
- Break up and mash salmon in a bowl
- Mix salmon with all ingredients

- Shape into a loaf or patties if desired
- Bake loaf at 350 degrees for 45 minutes
- Alternatively, fry patties in a little olive oil
- Serves 4

Grandma's Famous Potato Salad

Ingredients
- 6-8 large red potatoes
- 2/3 cup Miracle Whip Salad Dressing
- 4 hard boiled eggs, chopped
- ¼ cup sweet pickle relish
- 2 small sweet pickles
- ½ cup finely chopped onion
- 1 ½ cups chopped celery
- 1 tsp garlic powder
- Paprika

Preparation
- Peel potatoes, quarter and boil until done but not too soft
- Let potatoes cool, then cut into one inch cubes
- Add all ingredients to potatoes
- Mix thoroughly until potatoes are thoroughly coated with ingredients
- Refrigerate for a few hours before serving
- Sprinkle with paprika before serving
- Serves 6

Maizie's Baked Beans

Ingredients
- 2 cans quality pork & beans
- 2/3 cup ketchup
- 3 tbsp finely chopped onions
- 4 slices bacon

Preparation
- Drain most of the canned juice off the pork & beans
- Mix beans thoroughly with ketchup and onions
- Place mixture in baking dish

- Place bacon strips on top of bean mixture
- Bake at 350 degrees for one hour, checking periodically for burning
- Serves 6. Eat while hot!

The World's Best Party Dip!

Ingredients
- 16 oz. Philadelphia Cream Cheese
- 11/2 cups coarsely chopped green olives
- 1 cup thinly sliced ripe olives
- ¼ cup juice from green olive jar
- 1 tbsn. Worcestershire sauce
- 1 tbsn garlic powder (to taste—do you like garlic?)
- Sturdy dip chips or crackers (e.g., Townhouse)

Preparation
- Let the cream cheese soften naturally (or microwave on low setting)
- Mix cream cheese with all ingredients
- If more liquid is needed, use green olive juice
- Refrigerate for as long as possible
- Serve at room temperature with chips or crackers
- Serves 4-6

Breakfast Casserole

Ingredients
- Dozen eggs
- ½ cup milk
- 8 slices bread, cubed and dried
- 16 oz. grated cheddar cheese
- 1 pound breakfast sausage or Italian sausage if preferred
- Butter or no cal spray for bottom of baking dish

Preparation
- Cook and crumble sausage
- Spread bread cubes evenly in a greased 9x14 baking dish
- Beat eggs with milk
- Pour egg mixture evenly over bread

- Sprinkle sausage mixture over the top of the egg/break mixture
- Sprinkle shredded cheddar cheese over the entire mixture
- Bake at 350 degrees for 45-60 minutes (check doneness with toothpick)
- Let cool slightly, cut into squares, remove with spatula. Serves 4-6

Hodge Podge
(Army-Navy Memories!)

Ingredients
- Package frozen or refrigerated shredded hash browns, thawed
- 1 large onion, chopped in large pieces
- ½ green pepper chopped in large pieces
- 3 cloves fresh garlic, chopped
- 2 large pieces of Italian sausage, cut into medium slices (mild or hot, you decide)
- 6 eggs
- Salt and pepper to taste
- Olive oil or butter

Preparation
- Sautee onion, green pepper and garlic in large skillet containing olive oil/butter
- Add sliced sausage and brown
- Stir in hash browns
- Cook over medium heat for about 30 minutes, stirring frequently
- Salt and pepper to taste during cooking; add salt a little at a time
- Scramble the 6 eggs (add milk or cream if desired)
- Mix scrambled eggs with potatoes
- Serves 4.

Shroomed Pork Chops
(Simple but Delicious)

Ingredients
- 4 boneless pork chops
- 1 can condensed mushroom soup (e.g., Campbells)
- ¼ cup milk
- Salt & pepper

- Butter or no cal cooking spray

Preparation
- Trim excess fat from pork chops
- Place chops in a greased baking dish
- Mix mushroom soup with milk and pour evenly over the pork chops
- Bake until tender but not burned for about one hour at 350 degrees. Soup will become thickened. (Note: cooking time will be affected by thickness of chops

Caroline's Hearty Chili

Ingredients
- 3 pounds ground round
- 2 16-oz. cans kidney beans
- 32 oz can whole tomatoes
- 1 8 oz can tomato sauce
- 1 large onion
- 1 green pepper
- 1 tbls Garlic powder
- 3 tbls chili powder
- Salt & pepper
- Optional: Hot peppers such as chili peppers or jalapenos

Preparation
- Brown meat in a dutch oven/crumble meat as it cooks
- Chop tomatoes and add to meat
- Stir in tomato sauce
- Drain beans and add to mixture
- Add all other ingredients and stir thoroughly
- Simmer for 3 hours, stirring frequently
- Add chili powder and salt & pepper to taste. Don't overdo, you can add more at the end, but you can't remove it!
- For best flavor, let chili cool and refrigerate over night
- Heat or microwave before serving.
- Serve with options of diced onions, shredded cheddar, sour cream and sliced jalapenos. Serves

Wiffy's Beef Stew

Ingredients
- 2 pounds lean, quality stew meat, cut into cubes
- 2 large onions
- 16 oz fresh carrots cut into large pieces
- 4 pounds red potatoes
- 1 can beef broth
- Water
- 3 bay leaves
- 4 garlic cloves, smashed and diced
- Salt & pepper to taste
- Olive oil
- Optional: add can of peas and/or more carrots if desired

Preparation
- Brown meat in large dutch oven containing olive oil or butter
- Add onion and garlic, sauté
- Add bay leaves, 1 tsp salt, 1/8 tsp pepper
- Add liquids, bring to a boil
- Cook over medium heat for one hour
- Add carrots
- Simmer for one hour
- In a separate pan, boil potatoes, cut into large cubes and add to stew mixture
- Simmer for one more hour, stirring frequently. Add water as needed.
- Let potatoes decompose just enough to give stew some thickness
- Finish salt and pepper to taste
- Serves 4-6.

Great Grandma Jen's Sloppy Joes

Ingredients
- 2 pounds ground round
- 1 large onion, chopped
- 16 oz. can tomato sauce
- ¼ cup brown sugar

- 1 tbsn vinegar
- ¼ cup ketchup
- ¼ cup prepared mustard
- Hamburger buns

Preparation
- Brown meat in large skillet or dutch oven
- Add onion, cook five minutes, stirring
- Add balance of ingredients and stir well
- Simmer 1 hour
- Serve hot on bun with slice of onion or pickles if desired

###

www.ingramcontent.com/pod-product-compliance
Lightning Source LLC
Chambersburg PA
CBHW081128170426
43197CB00017B/2787